AF560833

THE NOVELS OF MULK RAJ ANAND

A New Critical Spectrum

THE NOVELS OF MULK RAJ ANAND

A New Critical Spectrum

Edited by
T.M.J. INDRA MOHAN

Published by

ATLANTIC

PUBLISHERS & DISTRIBUTORS (P) LTD

7/22, Ansari Road, Darya Ganj, New Delhi-110002
Phones : +91-11-40775252, 40775214, 23273880, 23275880
Fax : +91-11-23285873
Web : www.atlanticbooks.com
E-mail : orders@atlanticbooks.com

Branch Office: Chennai
Phones : +91-44-48531784, 28291383
E-mail : chennai@atlanticbooks.com

Printed & bound in India by Atlantic Print Services

Preface

Mulk Raj Anand is one of the literary heavy weights among the Indo-Aglian novelists, whose writing career spanned nearly four decades with immense output in a qualitative way. This book is intended to provide insight into the works of Anand in a broad-based manner. The essays in this collection are selected keeping in mind the requirements of students and teachers in the Indian and foreign colleges and Universities. This book is obviously not a formal treatise on Anand s novels but aims to give a detailed critical account of the writer from diverse sources. The book may therefore be used not only as a reference-text but also as a supplement to original texts. It is hoped that this comprehensive collection of critical essays, will be an adjunct to Anand s works in order to discern his writings in the right perspective.

Anand as a committed writer highlighted in his novels the burning social problems in down-to-earth terms. He had approached novels with missionary zeal to portray the sufferings of the downtrodden at the hands of the native rich people and the colonial rulers. He felt that his novels should inculcate in the minds of the people an awareness that they were subjected to double slavery in terms of casteism and poverty. Anand had brought out in unequivocal terms the plight of the masses at the hands of their masters and caste Hindus who together had created untold sufferings to them. Anand s novels chronicled the social maladies in India and he felt that they would be eradicated by following the foot steps of the great leaders like Gandhiji.

The present Volume is an exclusive anthology of writings on Mulk Raj Anand's literary output. The uniqueness of this anthology is the extensive Bibliography supplemented at the end. The various papers analyse in-depth the multifarious talents of Mulk Raj Anand's writing skills.

Binod Mishra's paper "Despair and Delight in the Novels of Mulk Raj Anand" shows how these two factors are an integral part of human life itself. Studying the characters of Bakha, Munoo and Gangu of Anand's first trilogy, the author portrays the deep despair and the arrested energy in these characters.

Shiv Kumar Yadav in "A Comparative Study of Mulk Raj Anand's *Untouchable* and Sharan Kumar Limbale's *Akkarmashi*" arrives at the conclusion that whether it is fiction or fact, *Akkarmashi* analyses universal set of miseries and *Untouchable* is just its subset.

Binod Mishra's paper "Identity Crisis in the Novels of Mulk Raj Anand" aims to seek the crisis of identity which Anand's characters suffer from, starting with Bakha's search for identity and steadfastness.

Ashok Kumar Bachchan in his paper entitled "Indian Nuances of Anand's English: An Examination of His Early Novels," presents an impressively long list of idioms, proverbs, abusive terms, expletives, swear words, imagery, symbols, similes, metaphors and translations of Indian languages into English.

"Mulk Raj Anand's *Untouchable*: A Triumph of Narrative Skill" by U.S. Rukhaiyar analyses the various tools of narration used by Anand such as point of view, focus, atmosphere, characterization and imagery.

The sufferings of an untouchable woman who refuses to remain a cow but rises up to her full stature by holding on to her convictions are presented in the article entitled "Humanistic Note: A Study in Mulk Raj Anand's *The Old Woman and the Cow*" written by Ramesh Kumar Gupta.

Ashok Kumar Bachchan, in his paper "Humour and Irony in the Pre-Independence Novels of Mulk Raj Anand," analyses the components of Humour and Irony. He shows how Anand has utilised these elements in his novels *Untouchable, Coolie, Two Leaves and a Bud, The Big Heart, The Village* and *Across the Black Waters.*

In his article "Individual versus Society in the Novels of Mulk Raj Anand and Anita Desai," Binod Mishra traces the impact of the restrictions imposed by society on individuals, as delineated in the works of the two novelists.

D. Ramakrishna leaves the trodden path of Anand's critics and studies the other facets of the novelist's genius, like art and cross-cultural studies, with special reference to *Across the Black Waters.* War and death are the special features of the analysis. Comparing Anand with Crane and Hemingway, Ramakrishna shows how Anand has universalised the horrors and the pity evoked by war.

T.M.J. Indramohan's "*Untouchable:* A Social Document" narrates how Mulk Raj Anand has treated the sensitive and inhuman subject in a lucid way making the novel even relevant to our times.

N.P. Ravikumar's "*Two Leaves and a Bud:* A Proletariat Novel," traces the various events that took place in the plantations during the British rule in India.

Evangeline Manickam Critically analyses *Coolie* as a fine literary evocation of a traditional social malaise.

The Anthology concludes with an extensive and impressive Bibliography of Primary Sources: Novels, Short Story Collections,

Books for Children, Non-fiction, Interviews, and Secondary Sources: Bibliographies, Special Issues, Books, Research Articles on Anand and his writings, Reviews and Dissertations.

I wish to thank all the contributors to this volume but for whose immense help this would not have become a reality. I thank sincerely Dr Gowri Sivaraman, Professor of English at D.G. Vainshna College, Chennai, who has been kind enough in helping me edit the book despite her heavy academic commitments.

My grateful thanks are due to Dr K.R. Gupta, Chairman of Atlantic Publishers and Distributors, New Delhi whose dedicated academic pursuit resulted in bringing out volumes of books on various aspects of British, American and Commonwealth literatures.

T.M.J. Indra Mohan

Contents

1

Despair and Delight in the Novels of Mulk Raj Anand

BINOD MISHRA

Mulk Raj Anand occupies an important niche in the field of Indian writing in English. An established novelist who deals in common and day-today themes of Indian villages and towns, makes it to the skyscrapers of cities enabling us to realize the chasm between two worlds. Starting his quest as a novelist with *Untouchable* hc musters enough guts to strengthen his characters to find their real fire in the furnace of fight for freedom. His simple characters smoulder within and keep the furnace burning till the fight comes to flames. A comparative look/observation of his characters between the first phase and the later phase makes our vision clear. An overall study of Anand s novels accentuates the fact that most of his works have taken birth in Despair and have perfected in Delight. An avid but hurried reader of novels may find Anand s works as boring and historical but a serious reader finds entering an ocean of joy with universal barrier of temporal sorrow.

The idea behind the title of this article is taken from the real chapters of life. Human life is a long and everlasting book where these two chapters are innately folded/unfolded and at times they override each other. One may find it as difficult to define delight and despair as to sweet and sour. But to my view, they can be illustrated with sunshine and shower, sun and slum, happiness and sorrow *et al.* My motive behind this coinage is to discover the same in the novels of Anand. Life moves on the two wheels of despair and delight which give a slice to our existence. Anand once told P.K. Rajan philosophically:

> Life does not admit itself to a linear approach. The approach is much more complex, incoherent, determined by instinct and emotion, impulse and idea.[1]

Since there are contradictory elements in Anand s personality, the growth of his consciousness is an existing drama for critics and scholars. His personal story can be viewed as the story of torments and ecstasies. The symbolic facts of his life are someway or the other related to his fictional impetus. Unconscious urges, repressions and fantasies colour his perception and imagination. The man who suffers is greater than the man who writes in the case of Anand. It is the personal despair and delight of Anand which is expanded in fictional terms. The fact that Anand is an optimistic humanist who can move the most pessimistic man to action [2] is a tribute to him.

Each novel of Anand has several layers of despair and delight. We hear in his fiction, echoes of all kinds. There are number of motivations in each of his novels. P.K. Rajan observes that the evolutionary Marxist comprehension of reality is enriched by a spiritual, metaphysical, lyrical quality in his novels. Each novel is a blend of despair and delight. K.R.S. Iyenger recognizes the genius of Anand when he remarks that Anand is a novelist who invokes a multitude of responses. [3]

It is difficult to discuss all the novels of Anand in this article. So, we shall analyze here the first trilogy and examine specific details to show how the energies of Anand s protagonists are arrested. Because Anand claims that like Shelley he has to stir the suppressed yearning for freedom and the forgotten inner rhythms and the natural biological urges for fulfilment. [4] Anand was keenly aware of the upward thrust of his protagonist. Independence for him is not only freedom from the alien rule but also the freedom from outworn, ethical fetters that bruised Indian spirit. Anand s pattern of despair and delight combines the most significant features of history, psychology and philosophy.

Anand s characters are born and bred in poverty. They are born to earn their own bread but the age-old tradition of keeping them under the yoke of dejection and debauchery born of exploitation deprive them of their dignity of labour. Historically they symbolize the labour class of pre-independent India but their exploitation by their masters is undoubtedly man s crime against man. The characters grow in an unhealthy environment of fear and fire but that does not negate their potential. The prevailing conditions of the ruler and the ruled, the high and the low eat up their flesh but not bones. Their persecution without their protest is the ample proof of their simplicity and innocence. But this shows their lack of education. Despair in the characters becomes an eye opener and prove to pave the way to delight. Years of depression and dejection have strengthened their bones and revolution seems at hand. Anand keeps the hope alive and when the characters grow to a full stature, he allows them to feel their guts that the ceremony on innocence won t be drowned.

Anand s first and his slim novel *Untouchable* (1935) shows the quintessential Anand. The hero of the novel Bakha is a child of darkness. The caste system which has degenerated with the passage of time into a hydra-headed evil signifies a set of crippling injunctions. Bakha lives in a cave-like dingy, dank, one-roomed mud-house. His features are handsome but sometimes knotted and ugly. His bones are stiff and his flesh numb with the cold. On the positive side, Bakha is in stature dignified, the nature s well-built child.

Anand presents in the life of Bakha an inauspicious day punctuated by happy and sad experiences. Bakha is confronted with a reality that s stripped off all romantic illusions. When he s slapped, he faces the crisis of identity. He is presented as a victim in a recalcitrant society. His various responses to the sad and happy incidence make the perspective of hope and despair complex. The remarks of Saros Cowasjee in this connection hint at the larger implications in perspective.

Untouchable opens quietly on an autumn morning and by the time the evening approaches, the author has been able to build round his hero a spiritual crisis of such breadth that it seems to embrace the whole of India. [5] When Bakha is slapped, he is full of despair. But it is not a moment of delight. Anand writes about his strength and rage in his soul. Anand writes: The accumulated strength of his giant body glistened in him with the desire for revenge while horror, rage indignation swept over his frame. [6]

Bakha s fondness for the sugary tea gave him delight. What delighted him more than the sugary tea or the sweeter memory of his mother was his work. Work was a sort of intoxication which gave him a glowing health and plenty of easy sleep. Apart from this darkening atmosphere, the sister of Ramcharan creates for Bakha a new world full of wonder and enchantment.

Neither Gandhi nor Christianity brings for Bakha the consolation and comfort he needs. It is only the poet who can give him a new vision to liberate him from his sickening surroundings. The novel does not end on a note of despair paralyzing the hero into inaction. The fires of the sunset blaze on the distant horizon. Bakha looks at the magnificent orb of terrible brightness blowing on the margin of the sky. The pattern of despair and delight is given a cosmic sweep in the concluding lines of the novel. Anand writes:

> As the brief Indian twilight came and went, sudden impulse shot through the transformation of space and time and gathered all the elements that were dispersed in the stream of his soul.[7]

Coolie comprehends deeper levels of despair and degradation with a subdued undercurrent of delight. The hero, Munoo, a frail boy in a hostile world moves from the village to the town, from the town to the city and then to the mountains broadening the canvas of the novel. He is eventually swept to his doom. He is more a victim than a rebel. Primitivism, capitalism, industrialism, communalism and colonialism are the various elements skilfully orchestrated into the novel. Life for Munoo is a test of his vitality and impetuosity and his fundamental right to happiness is denied to him in a hostile climate. The cotton mills in Bombay where the boy has to work exposes him to the full force of the callous capitalistic order. He drifts into a more complicated and devious world.

Munoo experiences savage struggle for survival. He has to endure the foul smell and stink, damp and sticky sweat, dust and heat and dung. In such a climate life is a despair and death a delight. The novel shows death through alienation. Despair is a pervasive feeling throughout the novel. But the element of delight is not absent. The novel is not unshaded by a touch of glamour. The glamour comes from the primitive emotions of the protagonist and the majestic sights of Nature.

Critics have viewed the Simla Chapter differently and they find it unrelated to the basic pattern. But Saros Cowasjee says forcefully that the hero must be retrieved from the horrors of Bombay. It is not without irony that the boy who comes from the hills merges into the hills after his death. The hills, streams, the waterfalls, the clouds, and crisp, cool air all stand in sharp contrast to the heat, humidity and heartlessness of Bombay. Anand does more than pint the infernal miseries of the helpless labourers who are morbidly fatalistic. Anand makes us feel the beauty and horror that lies beneath life s outer surface. [8]

We admire Munoo for his human and hedonistic impulses. His search for delight is menaced by the brutalizing urbanization symbolized by Bombay. He descends into the strange, airless outhouse and hears the deafening roar of the machine. There are demons outside him. Friendship and brotherhood do exist in the sickening climate of Bombay. What Bombay gives to the boy is only the congested streets and moonless sky. It is not without significance that his love for the high altitudes does not abate even in Bombay. The sudden surge of love and friendship makes the death of Munoo a memorable and moving moment.

Coolie may lack the economical and classical tightness of *Untouchable* as emphasized by Marlene Fisher but it does show movement, colour and restlessness. The fact that Munoo is sustained by his memories of childhood spent in the hills, his final return to his origin is not without positive significance. His death is not without deeper metaphysical significance. The transcendental close of the novel gives a new dimension to the context of despair and delight. When Munoo is torn from his moorings, his feeling of nostalgia for his lost world is not without delight. Anand writes:

> And through the tears, he could see the high rocks, the great granite hills, grey in the blaze of the sun and the silver line of the bees.[9]

Two Leaves and a Bud (1937) is a crucially important novel in the first trilogy, which deals with the theme of exploitation as a part of the larger colonial experience. There are oblique colonial references in the first two novels but in this novel colonialism is analyzed with greater concentration. The entire tragedy is unfolded against the dark backdrop of the tea plantation which symbolizes the might and inhumanity of the British empire. The racial problem looms larger in this novel. The Indian social life is given a new dimension. The British officials and their Indian subordinates are ranged against the defenseless coolies working in the stifling surroundings. The capitalist forces are symbolized in this novel by the British. The English men who believe in the ideology of whiteman s burden are pathologically suspicious of all Indians. Every coolie is a potential agitator for the British officials. The natural result of this distrust is the despair of the Indians working there.

Gangu, the main protagonist of *Two Leaves,* an old and infirm coolie works incessantly to keep his household oven burning. The poor working environment, with low dingy huts, without proper sanitary conditions is either a boon or bane for coolies. Notwithstanding their physical labour, some of the coolies have allowed their wives to warm the beds of their masters. This too is an endeavour to renew their identities since much depended upon the moods and temperaments of their masters. Gangu is much of an individual who s different from other coolies. His daughter Leila, too, conscious of her youth and beauty protests against Reggie Hunt s lust. Gangu tries to save his daughter from Hunt s orgies and is shot. Leila s mother dies in Gangu s arms crying for medicine. The sheer lack of a young man s courage and his faith to a system that has little concern for its followers, shatters Gangu s world. To my view, no novel of Anand is as painful as *Two Leaves* which fails to see the growth of a bud born and fated to be smashed and crushed by the crooked hands of a cruel class. The novel unfolds the story of anger and awe, cries and crimes with none to sympathize except the readers.

The strain of irony is unbearable at the close of the novel when Reggie Hunt who kills Gangu and attempts to defile his daughter is discharged. Marlene Fisher gives credence to this kind of perception in her following observation:

> Cruelty and oppression do win out in *Two Leaves and a Bud* leaving Anand sick with despair and rage.[10]

But Dr K.N. Sinha, on the contrary, feels that the novel derives its power from the counter pointing of good and evils Marlene Fisher loses sight of what is good and uplifting in the novel. Gangu is much more than a scapegoat sacrificed at the altar of the narrow racial prejudices. We can notice in the doctor the qualities which sharply contrast with the lust and cruelty embodied by Reggie Hunt. If the novel is viewed as a moral allegory, it means that the novel is not without dream and delight. We ought to remember that fiction is much more than straight facts.

Reggie Hunt may symbolize untamed animality and unmitigated evil, but he s alarmed at the rising force and expectation of the labourers working in the sickening surroundings. The following lines of the book give larger implications:

> The wild swing of their axes, the sharp sweep of their scythes, and the clean cut of their knives, filled Reggie with a belligerent passion for destruction.[11]

The sharp scythe in Leila s hand, the rustle of the breeze, the sweep of the grasses, the damp turbid smell of the sunless groves which creates an appropriate backdrop for the appearance of the python and its terrible embrace of Leila. After a good deal of writhing and wriggling, the sharp blade of Leila s instrument bruises the python. The blood on the scythes weaves together a number of emotions in the heart of the readers. The revolutionary message which is not without delight is transparent. Leila combines in her character turbulence and tenderness. Even Gangu is not too brutalized to respond to tragic situations in a deeply human manner. The novel assembles the humanistic, hellenistic and even the nihilistic impulses of the author and the protagonist of the novel.

It is thus evident that the energy of the protagonist in the first trilogy is arrested in the oppressive institutional framework. This arrest of energy in a web of prescriptions and prohibitions breeds in the hero a deep sense of despair. This cannot blind us to the sparks that occasionally flash in their soul. The social and political forces though formidable cannot black out the sun and stars for them. These heroes are aided in their search for coherence by the forces which are too big for the perpetuators of the cruel institutions to grasp. Delight which is like a faint glimmer appears with greater force in the second trilogy. This swing towards delight chiefly depends on the greater sense of the new hero s involvement and determination. The energy which is arrested in the first trilogy struggles relentlessly for its release in the second trilogy.

NOTES AND REFERENCES

1. P.K. Rajan, *Studies in M.R. Anand.*
2. S. Lakshman Shastri, Editorial, *Contemporary Indian Literature,* Nov.-Dec. 1965, 10.
3. K.R.S. Iyengar, Foreword to G.S. Balaramgupta s Book, Mulk Raj Anand: *A Study of his Fiction in Human Perspective,* Prakash Book Depot, 1974.
4. Mulk Raj Anand, *State Patronage of Art,* Cultural Forum, March-April 1963, 6.
5. Saros Cowasjee, *So Many Freedoms,* 10.
6. Mulk Raj Anand, *Untouchable,* 55.
7. *Ibid.*
8. Ira Morris, *Messages and Souvenirs, Contemporary Indian Literature,* Nov.-Dec. 1965, 9.
9. Mulk Raj Anand, *Coolie,* 24.
10. Marlene Fisher, *The Wisdom of the Heart,* 52.
11. Mulk Raj Anand, *Two Leaves and Bud,* 146.

2

A Comparative Study of Mulk Raj Anand s *Untouchable* and Sharan Kumar Limbale s *Akkarmashi*

SHIV KUMAR YADAV

Truth is always stranger than fiction is an age-old dictum. The relation between truth and fiction is somewhat like history and myth respectively as John Beattie explains, History and myth [...] are not the same, although there may be an element of history in myth, as there certainly is of myth in history. [1] Fiction like myth is weaved in and around fact, history and truth but also being governed by man (author) and milieu (environment). Mulk Raj Anand also opines in the similar vein: The novelist presumes to be God Almighty and indulges in the sport of creating a world of his own in his novel. [2] In order to have complete control over his puppets (characters), Anand declined the advice of Gandhi to write a straightforward pamphlet about Harijans.[3] The fictional form provides an ample opportunity to an author to be a deliberate victim of selective amnesia to justify his ways to his characters and viewpoints. On the other hand, an autobiographer who narrates his life s events and experiences, certainly within his own term and frame of references including his prejudice and bias, gives a transparent opportunity to a reader to get his story verified in the light of other sources of fact and truth *i.e.*, history.

This paper seeks to compare Mulk Raj Anand s *Untouchable,* a fiction and Sharan Kumar Limbale s *Akkarmashi* a fact (an autobiography), which narrate the plight and sufferings of a large segment of the Hindu society which acquired different names in different periods of the Indian history Antyaj or Chandals (exterior castes), Achoot (untouchables), Harijan (children of God), Scheduled Caste (a constitutional name), and now Dalit (depressed, a self-assumed socio-historical name). Anand s novels like *The Untouchable, The Coolie* and *The Big Heart* have been written with a motive to prop the economical and social questions of the Indian society. His Compassion for the Waifs, the disinherited, the lowly, the lost in a word Daridranarayan the Lord & incarnate Poverty) [4] is unquestionable. But his depiction of an untouchable in his *Untouchable* and the three solutions offered by him regarding the removal of untouchability, it seems to me, is just like touching the tip of an iceberg of the complex chronic and perhaps racial disease of Hindu collective consciousness, if it is compared with Limbale s *Akkarmashi.*

The *Akkarmashi,* originally written in Marathi and later on translated into Hindi by Dr Surya Narayan Ransubhe in 1991 depicts the agony and sufferings of Sharan Kumar Limbale in particular and of the Hindu untouchables in general. Limbale s description is so truthful and revealing that it belittles E.M. Forster s tall claim regarding Anand s *Untouchable.* Forster claims, *Untouchable* could only have been written by an Indian and by an Indian who observed from outside. No European, however, sympathetic could have created the character of Bakha, because he would not have known enough about his troubles. And no untouchable could have written the book, because he would have been involved in indignation and self-pity.[5] If Forster claims that however, sympathetic a European cannot create the character of Bakha, it can also be claimed in the line of his own logic that however compassionate, a Hindu caste cannot depict the plight and suffering of Sharan Kumar, an Akkarmashi, a word of Marathi means, in the words of Dr Ransubhe, Akkarmashi ka arth hai Jarajputra, Avaidh Santan, Samaj dwara amanya sambandho se janmi santati, istri ki majboori ko dekhkar, use rakhail bananewale sampann aur amanviya purush sambandho se janami santati, aisi santati ko marathi mein Akkarmashi kahte hain. [6] [Meaning of akkarmashi is love-child, Illicit-child, offspring born out of socially unacceptable relationship, offspring born out of a relationship in which a woman has been made a mistress by a well-do-do and inhuman person, by exploiting her helplessness. This sort of offspring is known as akkarmashi in Marathi.] This paper also attempts to underline the viewpoint that a participant observer (sufferer), despite the possibility of being victim of indignation and self-pity can reveal the truth and gauze the density of agony more pungently in comparison to non-participant observer (sympathiser).

Anand s *Untouchable* was germinated in early Twenties and published in 1935. And till today it has been published in thirty plus languages of the world, which certainly underlines its well deserved and unreserved acceptance everywhere. He wrote this novel, after being inspired by a poignant story about a sweeper boy, Uka, by Mahatma Gandhi in *Young India* written with the utmost simplicity. [7] Later on, he got his manuscripts heard by Gandhiji and after that pruned it to its extant size and contents. The influence of Gandhi on Anand is an open secret, but in *The Untouchable* he is so enchanted with Gandhism that he visualises the problem of untouchability thoroughly through the lens of Gandhi having few disagreements.

The Untouchable appeared nearly more than 50 years before *the Akkarmashi* but failed to capture the complete scene of sufferings of untouchables prevalent at that time. If we take the glimpses of painful experiences of Bakha, following significant incidents come to the fore: Morning abuse of his father (suar ka aulad, haramjada son of a pig, illegally-begotten); the slap on the face as he accidentally touched a caste Hindu, disapproving eyes of shopkeepers who sold jalebis to him, behaviour of charity bread giver woman; recollection of the story about the doctors refusal to give medicine to his father when Bakha was ill, the temple incident of Sohini and aftermath; Bakha s hesitation to take sweets from Ramcharan, abuse of the housewife because he carried her injured child home to her and so polluted the little one by his touch; quarrel between colonel Hutchinson and his wife when Bakha was brought to Colonel s residence. If we analyse these incidents of Bakha s life, it is very much clear that Anand s depiction revolves around the problem of untouchability practised by the Hindu Castes and their hypocrisy as well as untouchability among untouchables. The oblique reference of love-child of Gulabo Ramcharan, true son of his mother, Gulabo, if he wants his father s son, but of the richman, his mother s lover [8] by Anand shows his concern regarding the Hindu castes hypocrisy.

In the *Akkarmashi,* Sharan s story runs like this: Sharan, not only an untouchable but an akkarmashi also, belongs to Hannur village somewhere on the boundary of Maharashtra and Karnataka. His story begins from his maternal grandmother, Santamai, of Mahar caste, a deserted woman, having only one daughter the mother of Sharan Kumar, who lives with a Muslim, Mahmud Dastgir, referred as Dada by Sharan, within the framework of modern institution of live-in-relationship. Dada himself a deserted husband without any issue, lives with Santamai, as a committed partner, Masa Mai only daughter of Santa Mai from her first husband and mother of Sharan Kumar, marries Vithal Kamble of Baslegaon and gives birth of three sons. The eldest son dies very early. Hanmanta Limbale, as Patel of Baslegaon, under whose suzerainty Vithal Kamble works as an annual contract labour and receives Rs. 800, exploits the helplessness (due to acute poverty) of Vithal Kamble by making his wife his (Limbale s) mistress. In turn, he supports them in the rainy season. But it does not work for longer time and eventually Kamble deserts Masamai and deprives her of two sons. Masamai does not marry again. Hanmanta Limbale likes her decision and makes a separate arrangement of her at Akkalkot, where Sharan appears on this earth as an Akkarmashi. Later on, disenchantment grows in Limbale, and he starts levelling accusations of being faithless against Masamai so the paternity claim of Sharan Kumar can be disowned. Being mentally agonised of his accusations and tortured of atrocities, she returns to her mother Santamai along with Sharan. Here Sharan grows under the unconditional love of Santamai and her live-in-partner Dada, Mahamud Dastgir, and also collects his experiences as an untouchable as well as an Akkarmashi. Masamai, here, again becomes mistress of another touchable Yashwant Sidramappa Patel, a prominent person of Hannur village, where they live, and gives birth of eight more akkarmashi six females and two males. Sharan obtains his

Bachelor Degree in 1978 and gets appointment for the post of Telephone Operator. Sharan writes in the preface of The Akkarmashi his autobiography Mere Saale Subhash Ki Atmakatha bhi isi prakar ki hai. Uski Maa Achoot, Pita Berar Samaj Ka. Pita Amir, Mahanagarpalika Ka Sadasya; Aur Maa? Mahanagarpalika Ki Chaturth Shreni Ki Majdoor Aurat.[9] [Biography of my brother-in-law is the same. His mother, an untouchable, father from Berar society. The father rich, a member of Metropolitan Council, and the Mother? fourth grade woman labour of Metropolitan Council.] This is not the story of Sharan, it is only his genealogy and chronology. As a matter of fact his story of sufferings and miseries is the story of an untouchable of the post-independent, democratic republic, secular and socialistic India. Despite several constitutional and legal measures initiated by the State still we have a number of Sharan and Subhash.

The story of Bakha in the *Untouchable,* it seems to me, is just a struggle for emancipation from the sufferings of untouchability while the *Akkarmashi* apart from being a struggle for emancipation from the human bondage, it is also a craving quest for identity. Mathematically, we can say that if the Akkarmashi is almost universal set of miseries, the *Untouchable* just its subset. In the description of every incident, Sharan shows the injuries and scars caused by glaring discriminations and atrocities perpetuated by the caste Hindus. Space limitation does not permit to narrate all the painful experiences of Sharan s life here, but few incidents need to be described. In the very beginning, we find how the students of untouchable community enjoy the left-over, remnants and droppings of the touchable at the end of the picnic. When Sharan describes this incident of the picnic, his mother, Masamai, complains Ghar ke logo ke liye usme se thoda le aata to kya bigarta? Bacha hua anna amrit hota hai.[10] [It wouldn t have caused you any harm if you would have brought some of that (droppings) for we people. The droppings are like nectar.] Another event also clearly shows the acute poverty prevalent among untouchables. Sharan narrates: Fasal ke dino mein janwar jyada kha lete. Jwar ke bhutte khane ke bad unke gobar mein phule huae dane dikhte, Dano mein bhare huae aise gobar ko Santamai alag se rakhati. Ghar lautate samay raaste mein nadi ke pani mein us gobar ko Santamai dhoti. Gobar nikal jata, dane alag ho jate. Maa un dano ko sukhati. Sukhane ke bad woh kam ho jate. Mujhe lagta, unhe sukhana hi nahi chahiye, Sukhane ka bad to we kam ho jate. Dane sukhane ke bad hum ghar lautate. Un dano ko woh chakki mein khud peesti, gati hui."[11] [In the harvesting season, cattle would eat more than they could digest. The undigested grains were visible in the dung. Santamai would keep such dung separately, while returning home, Satamai would clear the dung in the river water. Thus gains and dung would get separated. Maa would dry the grains. The amount of grains would get lessened after being dried. It seems to me, that must not be dried as it would get lessened. We would return home after having dried the grains. She would grind the grains herself while singing in the grinding stones.] Here we find even animals are more fortunate than the untouchables who get more fodder than they needed. Sharan narrates further that Santamai would never give the bread of those grains to him and his brothers and sisters. She alone would consume those pieces of bread. They would eat "Chani"-dried pieces of carrion when they would have scarcity of food. Stones would serve the purpose of bath-soap and alkaline soil as detergent. Sharan would use the soap-lather floating in the river, but only on the condition that he would help the person from whose clothes soap-lather floats.

Sharan's story impels one to analyse the reasons responsible for the sub-animal status of untouchables in our society. Sharan, even, cannot claim his lineage among untouchables as his biological father is a Patel, a Savarna. Savarna calls him an untouchable and the untouchable calls him an "akkarmashi." We come across a situation when the two Patels—the father of Sharan and the father of other brothers and sisters Limbale and Sidramappa visit Masamai together. She is unwilling, but Sidramappa wants that she should share bed with Limbale for the night. Is Masamai more than an animal?

The revelation of facts regarding the conditions of untouchables in the "Akkarmashi" questions the efficacy of the three solutions to the problem of untouchability offered

As a matter of fact, Anand himself rejects the first option as it is evident when Bakha recalls his father s reaction regarding the change of faith [...] that he had refused to leave the Hindu fold, saying that the religion which was good enough for his forefathers was good enough for him. [12] Further, again, To Bakha [...] the few words which she (wife of the Colonel) had uttered carried a dread a hundred times more terrible than the fear inspired by the whole tirade of abuse by the touched man. [13] Regarding the other two solutions, Bakha is duly impressed, feels more hopeful of the future than at any time since the day dawned, and returns to his house to tell his father about the Mahatma and about the machine that will clear dung without anyone having to handle it. [14] Very promptly, E.M. Forster appears in support of Anand to justify his solutions, when he says, It is the necessary climax, and it has mounted up with triple effect. Bakha returns to his father and his wretched bed, thinking now of the Mahatma, now of the Machine. His Indian day is over and the next day will be like it, but on the surface of the earth if not in the depths of the sky, a change is at hand. [15] *The Akkarmashi* appears in the Nineties, and cries loudly where is the change.

Gandhi fails to understand the problem despite this, Bipin Chandra writes, experience in South Africa was unique in one respect. By virtue of being a British-educated barrister, he demanded many things as a matter of right, such as first class tickets and rooms in hotels, which other Indians before him had never probably even had the courage to ask for. Perhaps, they believed that they were discriminated against because they were not civilized that is westernized. Gandhiji s experiences, the first of a westernized Indian in South Africa, demonstrated clearly to him and to them that the real cause lay elsewhere, in the assumption of racial superiority by the white rulers. [16] The same experienced Gandhi tries to see the problem of casteism and untouchability as an unrelated issue, and according to him, certainly not rooted in the Varnashram as it is not found in Hindu s original scriptures. He assumes untouchability just a deviance so its eradication is sufficient enough to ensure all sort of justice to the untouchable. Probably, he could not see that the caste names of untouchables are the words of abuse for the touchables. Arundhati Roy underlines this agony of untouchables in her masterpiece, They were also demanding that untouchables no longer be addressed by their caste names. They demanded not to be addressed as Achoo Paravan or Kelan Paravan, or Kuttan Pulayan, but just as Achoo, or Kelan, or Kuttan. [17] If untouchability has its physical dimension only, then how does Gulabo and Masamai become the mothers of the touchables. And being a confirmed believer of his own assumption, his Harijan campaign included a programme of internal reform by Harijan, promotion of education, cleanliness and hygiene, giving up the eating of carrion and beef, giving up liquor and the abolition of untouchability among themselves. [18] Even Anand differs from Gandhi although very mildly. When Bakha hears Gandhi saying, In order to emancipate themselves they have to purify themselves. They have to rid themselves of evil habits, like drinking liquor and eating carrion [19] he felt, That is not fair. [20] Gandhi does not see that, In fact, Sanskritisation depends upon resource availability, mobilisation and accessibility at the level of the lower castes [21] and the sankritising castes may even face a threat or challenge from the dominant castes. [22]

The Third solution Machine certainly brings a change in the physical dimension of untouchability but what about its psychological dimension. A comrade in *The God of Small Things*, speaks, But frankly speaking, comrade, Change is one thing, Acceptance is another. [23] Sharan Kumar goes to another village for hair-cutting where his identity as an untouchable is not known to the barber.

Bakha is a fictional character while Sharan, a living individual. Sharan Limbale could have written his own story in fictional form and then might have ensured enough scope and freedom to make his story an epic of sufferings of untouchables of India as a whole. But Sharan just narrates his story and never tries to visit the past saving few anecdotes of Santamai and others, nor visualise the future. And that s why like Bakha who is only partly the prototypical untouchable, for he is also himself, a unique individual, even in some measure in exceptional untouchable. [24] Sharan is also an untouchable not the untouchable but his story comes very close to the sufferings of untouchables as a whole cutting across the regions of India. Sexual exploitation of the untouchable woman by the touchable man has been prevalent in every part of India. Sexual exploitation of tenant of womenfolk was rampant to such an extent particularly in Masaurha Zamindari, that the foremost peasant leader of Bihar in the Zamindari period, Swami Sahajanand Saraswati notes in his autobiography Mere Jeevan Sangarsh (My Life Struggle), that tenants outside Masaurha were unwilling to get their daughters married there. [25]

Comparing the intensity and density of sufferings of untouchables described in the *Untouchable* and the *Akkarmashi,* the later seems to be the story of the Twenties or even more earlier while the former is of the Sixties and Seventies. The *Untouchable* has earned a worldwide publicity and evoked sympathy for untouchables, but I wonder, no one questioned that it was very less than the reality. Bakha once suffers from spiritual nausea, when he learns that he is the cause of the mem-sahib s anger,[26] but I perceive, this, as the spiritual nausea of Anand s learned humanism. Similarity does exist between Bakha and Sharan and that is of helplessness, self-pity and indignation, throughout the narratives of Anand and Limbale.

The *Untouchable* ends with some solutions, as Anand perceives the whole things only externally and mechanically as an observer, but the *Akkarmashi* ends with the baptism of Sharan s son. Sharan gives a name Anarya as he perceives the whole things culturally and psychologically as a sufferer hence wishes to return to his historical or mythical root as even after many millenniums, his integration could not get completed into the Aryans fold despite Gandhiji s long fasting before the Poona pact.

REFERENCES

1. John Beattie s *Other Culture,* Routledge & Kegan Paul, 1964, 24.
2. Mulk Raj Anand s, *Untouchable,* Arnold Associates, 1981, 181.
3. *Ibid.*
4. K.R. Srinivas Iyengar s *Indian Writing in English,* Sterling Publishers, New Delhi, 332.
5. E.M. Forster s Preface to the *Untouchable* by Mulk Raj Anand, 9.

6. Sharam Kumar Limbale s Akkarmashi [Translated edition (Hindi), Granth Akademi, New Delhi, 199], 5.
7. Mulk Raj Anand s *Untouchable*, Arnold Associates, 1981, 179.
8. *Ibid.*, 99.
9. Sharan Kumar Limbale s Akkarmashi [Translated edition (Hindi), Granth Akademi, New Delhi, 1991], 9.
10. *Ibid.*, 14.
11. *Ibid.*, 23.
12. Mulk Raj Anand s *Untouchable*, Arnold Associates, 1981, 138.
13. *Ibid.*, 149.
14. *Ibid.*, 173.
15. *Ibid.*, 10.
16. Bipin Chandra s *India□s Struggle for Independence*, Penguin India, 1992, 172.
17. Aundhati Roy s *The God of Small Things*, India Ink, 1998, 69.
18. Bipin Chandra s *India□s Struggle for Independence*, Penguin India, 1992, 294.
19. Mulk Raj Anand s *Untouchable*, Arnold Associates, 1981, 165.
20. *Ibid.*
21. K.L. Sharma s *Indian Society*, NCERT, 1987, 145.
22. *Ibid.*
23. Aundhati Roy s *The God of Small Things*, India Ink, 1998, 279.
24. K.R.S. Iyengar s *Indian Writing in English*, Sterling Publishers, 338.
25. A.N. Das s *The Republic of Bihar*, Penguin India, 1992, 122.
26. Mulk Raj Anand s *Untouchable*, Arnold Associates, 1981, 149.

3

Identity Crisis in the Novels of Mulk Raj Anand

BINOD MISHRA

> Man s fate, today, is no longer in the hands of the gods, but is often in conflict with the evil in other men. Man makes himself, or thinks he can. The heart and mind of contemporary man is, therefore, moved by other casualties than salvation.[1]
>
> *Mulk Raj Anand*

Mulk Raj Anand, one of the triumvirates of the established Indian writers during the alien rule on our native land draws in characters from our everyday experiences presents them as they are. Not many authors before him could realize the importance of these non-entities and sympathize with their private tears and cheers. The unjust social and political order debases the qualities of human heart in his early novels. But this is only a fragment in his fiction. His hero in each novel shows courage and resilience and emerges from darkness and disruption.

The present paper aims to seek the crisis of identity Anand s characters suffer from. The pangs and suffering of his fictional figures bear the stamps of Anand who suffered the tedium of an empty and banal life where growth and self-awareness were thwarted. He writes with anguish that he grew up in a small world, materially poor and spiritually limited. His mother s influence permeated the very core of his being whereas his father s subservience gave him unmitigated despair. His university days were not happy. The murder of Yashmin, his beloved with whom he wanted to elope with, deepened his despair. Foreign rule pricked his conscience. He was jailed for his campaign in 1921. He disgraced his family and his father fretted. Anand decided to go to England to escape from despair.

Anand tries to seek the causes of identity crisis in his characters. He s very close to Shelley who recognized man existing both as a social being and an imaginative individual. To exist meant for Shelley a life lived in two worlds, the outer and the inner. Anand, like Shelley believes that every individual is an imaginative being and it s his imaginative mind that always seeks its identity with the universal system of things.

Anand s literary pilgrimage began with *Untouchable* (1935). The novel describes a day in the life of Bakha, a scavenger a well-built child of nature. His beautiful physical features have few takers. He becomes a victim of the prevailing caste-system during pre-independent India. The entire novel is the description of only one day when Bakha is slapped and for the only reason that he belonged to a low caste. The colony in which Bakha lives is dark and deep. When Bakha is slapped, he faces a crisis of identity. Critics may find the novel to be an attack on the caste-system but then it s also an individual s struggle against a sea of dogmas. Anand allows Bakha to confront with a reality that s stripped of all romantic illusions. The crisis of identity that Bakha faces characterizes and colours the personality of Bakha by his unquenchable wonder at life.

Bakha is a child of darkness, no doubt, but he derives his strength from the sun. His enormous capacity for work makes each muscle of his body shine forth like glass. He has his desires and dreams too. He, like every individual, longs for his identity. Anand describes the violent stirring in the soul of Bakha very candidly:

> The accumulated strength of his giant body glistened in him with the desire for revenge while horror, rage, indignation swept over his frame.[2]

Dr C.D. Narasimhaiah discovers in each novel of Anand human centrality. He firmly affirms that *Untouchable* is not a propaganda piece because Bakha fights to seek his identity and steadfastness.

Bakha s bones are stiff and his flesh numb. But it does not numb his private feeling. His burning flames give him a sense of power. There are sores in his soul and his sense of segregation is corrosive. One can hear Bakha s self-cry in the following lines:

> But the crowd which passed round him, staring, pulling, grimacing, jeering and leering was without a shadow of pity for his remorse.[3]

D. Reimenschender explores the problem of labour and fulfilment from a different angle. Since most of the Anand s heroes labour, it is viewed as an instrument of self-realization. If man is alienated from the product of labour it s a moment of despair. Reimenschneider remarks:

> If man is alienated from his own nature, he is also alienated from the human nature of his fellow beings a fact most obvious in the existence of antagonistic classes within a society.[4]

Perhaps the sugary tea which Bakha drank every morning, provided him with some fond experiences. More than the sweet tea and the sweet memory of his mother was his work, which gave him some triumph. Bakha s fight for his identity and survival get some consolation when the sister of Ramcharan creates for Bakha a new world full of wonder and enchantment. Bakha s feelings for that girl have been very graphically described in the novel:

> There was something wistful about her, a soft light in her eyes for which she had become endeared to him. She had grown up to be a tall girl with a face as brown as ripe wheat and hair as black as the rain clouds.[5]

Bakha is trapped and is a victim of a recalcitrant society and he needs neither Gandhi nor Christianity but the poet who gives him a new vision to liberate him from his sickening surroundings.

The other two novels of the first trilogy, *Coolie* and *Two Leaves* also run on the theme of exploitation and raise the question of identity crisis of their protagonists. Munnoo, the protagonist of coolie moves from the village to the town, from the town to the city and then to the mountains broadening the canvas of the novel. More extensive in time and space than the first novel, *Coolie* has an edge over *Untouchable.* Munnoo s experiences in Bombay and Daulatpur emphasize his savage struggle for survival. He endures the foul smell and stink, damp and sticky sweat, dust and heat and dung. Munnoo is a fragile boy in a hostile world. Life for him is a test of his vitality and impetuosity and his fundamental right to happiness is denied to him in a hostile climate. The cotton mills in Bombay where the boy has to work exposes him to the full force of the callous capitalistic order. He drifts into a more complicated and devious world. Munnoo represents the labour class and suffers the infernal miseries of the helpless labourers who are morbidly fatalistic. His cry for his identity is silenced by the deafening roar of the machine. It is not without irony that Munnoo is not willing to tear himself away from the sandy margins where he ran to the tune of lavish beauty. It is also not without irony that he traces the outlines of Sheela s figure with a delicate light on her regular mobile features. Munnoo s impetuosity, the utter humanness of his impulses, the sheer wantonness of his unconscious life force reveal his natural vitality. Munnoo dies and his death is a memorable and moving moment.

> Munnoo clutches at Mohan s hand, felt the warm blood in his veins like a tide reaching out to distance to which it had never gone before.[6]

The opening line of the novel *Two Leaves and a Bud* Life is a journey into the unknown hints at the crisis that it s packed with. The hero of the novel Gangu, an old and beaten man becomes a victim of colonial exploitation. The tragedy of the novel is unfolded against the dark backdrop of the tea plantation, which symbolizes the might and in-humanity of the British Empire. The coolies live in stifling surroundings and are part of the larger colonial experience. Gangu becomes a victim of man, god and civilization. He faces the storm, which ruins his harvest and shakes his identity. His wife dies in the lack of medical facilities and his world is broken. Even Gangu himself is killed while trying to save his daughter Leila from being defiled. His entire life is a saga of struggle and every moment he tries to safeguard his identity but fails. Much more than a scapegoat he sacrifices himself at the altar of the narrow racial prejudice. But he is not without zeal and zest for life. Anand writes:

> He gripped the handle of his spade with an wavering faith and dug his foot into the sod made by a furrow and sensed the warm freshness of the earth that would yield fruit.[7]

Anand allows his characters to be more experienced in the second trilogy called Lalu-trilogy. The crisis of identity in this trilogy gains momentum and the claim for recognition becomes more extensive and existential. Where Bakha s crisis is born out of personal cry Lalu s is for broad identity. He becomes more of a patriot than a personal being and advocates for the release of his motherland from the clutches of an alien rule. The author in Anand who allowed his character in the first trilogy an arrest of energy, makes them struggle for release which will pave the path to freedom and joy. We find his characters maturing and educating themselves in the process of struggle and self-discovery. Anand, who gives voice to the voiceless, is of the belief that years of depression and dejection have strengthened their bones and a revolution seems at hand. He instills a hope in them as they grow to a full stature; he makes them realize that the ceremony of innocence won t always be drowned.

The Village (1939), *Across the Black Waters* (1941), *The Sword and the Sickle* (1942) deal with Lalu s despair. He is a young rebel bubbling with energy and vibrating with dreams and determined to reject all the prohibitions and prescription of the conservative Indian society. His haircut is considered as the worst kind of transgression. His crushed identity forces him to run away from his society and join the war as a professional soldier in the second novel. But his dreams are frustrated and his experiences strengthen his desire for introspection and exploration. The third novel, *The Sword and the Sickle* (1942) concludes Lalu s quest for self-actualization and self-realization on a note that is not rigidly ideological. When Lalu comes back to his country, he find its furrowed face unrecognizable. Lalu reconciles himself to his fate. He s imprisoned for his rebellion and from the jail he gives his countrymen the message of love, non-violence and togetherness. His despair is the result of the constant awareness of a split in his consciousness. He is shocked to realize that he is also a victim of the age-old inheritance. Lalu faces the fury of his father and his hair cut is viewed as the most terrible insult to his religion.

The basic question that gives a sharp focus to the whole gamut of Lalu s experiences is the question about his identity and destiny, which cannot be separated from his despair and delight. Lalu is in a constant state of tension because he is determined to rebel against the unthinking, unfeeling hierarchy perpetuated by vested interests in India. He is different from the ostracized Bakha or the pensive Munnoo or the aged and ineffectual Gangu. If Anand underrates the conscious factor and presents the revolutionary hero in a sketchy manner, he is not willing to succumb to the facile victory that characterizes the Marxist literature. What is more important for Anand is the question of survival, which absorbs all the energy of his hero. The second trilogy is more epical containing the whole gamut of human experience with the dynamic hero at the centre. Moreover, the trilogy emphasizes forcefully the reassertion of faith in the struggle to live, to grow and to fight for survival. Lalu is able to re-organize his personality and the important part of his mission is that the individual has to be saved. Lalu tempers his youthful recalcitrance and the constant process of introspection has its share of despair and delight. R. Shepherd very perceptively remarks:

> Lalu s dilemma is one of conflicting loyalties. He is torn between past errors, the present commitments and the future aspiration.[8]

Lalu s attitude to Gandhi shows his despair because he does not share the superhuman qualities prescribed by Gandhi for the salvation of mankind. All the lofty notions of Gandhi like suffering; soul-force self-perfection and sublimation are alien to the exuberant and turbulent self of Lalu. Terrorism is as disgusting to Lalu as self-righteousness. What gives Lalu real joy is love and understanding which is more important and more effective than any political or religious dogmas. He knows that only Maya could give him the pulsing warmth in a world vitiated by caution, fear and resentment. We find in the given lines how the private and the public concerns create a tension in his character:

> Perhaps he felt there was nothing concrete in the outside world to cling to. He had never really becomes master of himself, of his destiny and was susceptible to all the weaknesses in his nature.[9]

The Big Heart (1945), *The Road* (1963) and *The Death of a Hero* are also dominated by the young protagonists who symbolize the spirit of joy. Though the characters in these novels also undergo sickness, morbidity and enertia but every moment of their life is strewn with despair. Anant in *The Big Heart* lives in a village which is a confusing jumble of the old and the new beliefs. He symbolizes the new upsurge in opposition to the old orthodoxy. The identity crisis in this novel gains a wider scope and Anant s revolutionary ideas are for the welfare of the whole and not of his own alone. Anant becomes the victim of Ralia s untamable fury and is killed. Ralia s vindictive passion and malice are the result of his ignorance. Anant symbolizes each impulse of life and tries to master his destiny by battling with the despair and abolishing unnecessary suffering. There are cankers in his soul but he keeps a vigilant eye on them. He was determined to outflank his destiny and his commitment to truth was absolute. His commitment was not only to himself but also to those who, like him suffered the crisis of identity. We can note the sores in his soul:

> No God, he felt could make such a world and consign it to such suffering for if he did so, he was not a good God.[10]

The crisis of identity acquires cosmic proportion in this novel. What Anant symbolizes in human and spiritual terms is more important than the way he is destroyed. Anant s trust in the here and now, his faith and pity and compassion and recognition of the dignity of man delights the reader. The irrational desires of the people the fears, the prejudices and the suspicion are the real threats to the joy of the individual. Anand laments that the individual is in a mouse-trap. He allows the protagonist to express his crisis:

> Caught in the mouse-traps where they are born, most of them are encaged in the bigger cage of fate and the various indiscernible shadows that hang over their heads.[11]

Bhikhoo in *The Road* is a victim of casteism. More organized and articulate than Bakha, Bhikhoo too faces the crisis of identity. But he symbolizes a climate of new togetherness. It's a moment of joy and consolation to him that Rukmini, the landlord's daughter responds to his love even in the face of hostility from her society. She rages against her father and brother who bring the disaster to the untouchables. Bhikhoo's crisis gets some moment of relief in the silent steady gaze of Rukmini.

Death of a Hero (1964), dealing with the disruption and disorientation and the communal frenzy, shows its protagonist's idea of death because he knows that the blind orthodoxy will frustrate all his positive and humanistic ideas and idealism. The novel shows Maqbool's consciousness of his identity. He is self-willed and not "wrapped up in the symbols of religious negation." The agonizing awareness of fear and hostility makes him passive and pensive. Maqbool fights the monsters and dies a glorious death. He symbolizes a new myth without which national resurgence cannot have any meaning. As a poet it is his mission to fire the imagination of the whole nation. His suffering is coloured with a longing of the welfare of humanity. He tells his sister:

> It is a question of faith, of belief in ourselves and in the struggle. And then we can hope to be free. We shall have to suffer and suffer but that is how man grows.[12]

Maqbool's letter found from his pocket after his death records his dreams of the nation and the heroic deeds of the people. All this for him constitutes the heritage of struggle. Dr Balram Gupta describes Maqbool's death as the harbinger of real triumph. Maqbool can be viewed as a positive image because he has the radiance of an unrepressed joy in contrast to the inward darkness of Bakha, Munnoo and Gangu. He emphasizes the urge for freedom from the heritage of struggle and the love of life.

We find echoes of identity crisis in the novel *Private Life of an Indian Prince* (1953) but in different way. The hero of the novel Vicky brings crisis in his life because of his own infirmities. His despair is rooted in the various strains that remain unrecognized in his personality. He is a pathetic captive of the changing colours of enchantress Gangi s moods. The colours of her lust and passion give the prince unending thrill and excitement. The enchantress puts a new zest into the banal life of the prince. What brings crisis for the prince is his enormously enlarged ego, which remains unappeased in the newly emerging democratic climate of the country. The inner and outer disruption, the cancer of doubt, and the lack of stable temperament paralyze the prince. It s the thwarted love of the prince for the hill woman that gives him pangs and despair. It is not without irony that his emotion for the woman does not grow into a bright creative aura. The pull of carnal desire may be normal but what is abnormal is the ugly fact that Gangi is coiled up in the entails of the prince. The story of the prince illustrates that we have a large heritage of darkness in the subterranean caves of our nature. What gives despair to Anand is the lack of will and the lack of creative purpose in life. The madness of the prince may be a complex event but it is not positive. The prince is destroyed by the dark seething waves that well up from the within. Vicky s suffering according to Dr K.N. Sinha, is without delight because it is not transformed into spiritual torment. The prince brings for himself only despair because his madness is not lit up by the glimmer of self-knowledge. Apart from Vicky s personal despair the novel is a study of man s dreams and desires as stated forcefully by Dr Shankar, his friend physician:

> I believe in men. They have a great vitality, in spite of humiliation they have suffered. I do not believe that there is a soul distinct from the body. The soul is the body and the body is the soul and together they make a man. Mysticism is the approach of a dying man. Man is the final fact of the universe. There is nothing higher than human existence. I do not believe there is any power transcending man who decides things for him.[13]

Anand lived in an age that threatened the individual s sense of personal meaning. He wrote autobiographical novels to secure that sense of self. The problem of identity was for Herbert Read, an effective death protest against the permeating power of collective death-wish. His autobiographical novel breaks the vice of reticence and overwhelms the readers with the expressive emotional honesty in all the four volumes *Seven Summers* (1951), *Morning Face* (1968), *Confessions of a Lover* (1976) and *The Bubble* (1984). His confessions in these novels are secularized rather than sacramental. Individuation and not salvation is his central pre-occupation in these novels. Everything is subordinated to the act of self-exploration and self-actualization. Anand raises a cluster of awkward questions about authentic living, which divorces itself neither from pain nor from pleasure.

Anand is at his best in expressing the identity crisis in his autobiographical novels. It is in them that he puts joys and sorrows of his heart. His earlier novels may have their epical range but their framework hindered the novelist from unlocking the secret of his heart. His autobiographical novels enable the collective consciousness of India. Anand confesses candidly:

> The connection between my life and writing is more intimate than in other novelists. I write as I live. My life is my message.[14]

Anand choose Krishan as the protagonist of his autobiographical novels. Krishan s acquaintance with the world, which offers him attraction and distractions and also challenges gradually deepens his vision of life. The rose buds and the scratches of the thorns were the sweet and bitter experiences of the growing child. Death as a dark reality hovers menacingly in the opening pages of the novel *Seven Summers* (1951). The outbursts of Krishan s feelings have the ample proof of an individual s crisis:

> I closed the eyes against Prithvi s face that seemed to be coming towards me from a far land he had gone nearer and nearer, for I was sure that he would return. Darkness descended on me. Sleep. There was nothing more.[15]

Krishan lives in a precarious, fragile world full of silences. Turbulence and silence are the two poles showing his identity. The child always symbolizes terrific high spirits. The earth and the sky grew bigger and bigger for him during those days. His eyes were consumed by the dreads and fantasies. Even the dissolute fields overgrown with cactus and stubble fascinated him. Krishan is a growing child responding to the changing situations of life with uncommon courage and candour. He dismisses disdainfully his father as a patched-up compromise of the mechanistic Europe and feudalist Asia. The father could not analyze the feelings of his son because the struggle for existence had ruined his sensitivity. Krishan hated his mother in her sacred mood of worship because she looked distant and detached.

Anand dispenses with the third person narrative method in his autobiographical novels and adopts confessional method to capture the colour and texture of the protagonist s emotions and thoughts. There is a definite process of development in his fiction. The growth of self-awareness takes a more definite shape in *Morning Face* (1968). The protagonist enacts the drama of existence in its love-hate relationship in the phenomenal world. The panoramic background of struggling India adds to the pattern of identity crisis a new dimension. The focus in the novel is, however, fixed on the protagonist and his evolution to higher consciousness. The clash of faiths in the home of protagonist shakes his identity. He does not respect the sane suggestions of his father, breaks the curfew and is punished for that. The merciless massacre at Jallianwallah Bagh completely alienates him from father. Anand describes his anguish in the following lines:

> I now began to realize acutely the nature of difference between the two worlds in which I lived, the world of the compromise of my father and the world of the principles of the nationalist.[16]

This is symbolic of the clash between tradition and change. Krishan looks for an outlet for expressing the energy of volcano latent in his being. His aggressive egoism expresses itself in his campaign against the elders, against the supreme God and against his father.

The death of Kaushalya is the first crack in the consciousness of the adolescent protagonist. The marriage of his elder brother is for him is an institutionalized suppression. Krishan s despair is deepened by women in this novel. Devaki, Mumtaz and Shakuntala nourish the protagonist emotionally. Krishan loved Shakuntala for her courage and candour in a climate of sycophancy and hypocrisy. She gave sustenance to his emotional life. Krishan s quest for love gradually transforms itself into his quest for truth. His struggle for achieving a new identity continues in his confession of a lover with greater force and unrelenting tenacity. He is determined to resurrect his self. He has to distill all his experiences into a metaphysical pattern. What Iqbal says in his *Secret of the Self* stirs up the consciousness of Krishan in a profound way. Anand takes Iqbal s admonition with all sincerity and seriousness:

> Read, read everything that comes your way. You can grow, everyone can. Only life and more life. Taste it and see it. It is bitter sweet.[17]

Self-awareness is, for Krishan, not an escape but a way of grappling with the world. It is his experience of love, its despair and delight that widen his consciousness. The love between a Hindu boy and a married Muslim woman has various ramifications. When Krishan loves Yashmin, he finds in her all the beauty and moisture of the earth and water.

Anand shows his exuberance and zest for life fully in his internationally acclaimed novel *The Bubble* (1984) wherein Krishan s consciousness is wafted into new areas. Krishan s identity as an Indian, who is not prepared to annihilate his root, is shaken. His encounters with a number of situations and personalities give him the best kind of education in England. What gave him dread and despair is the split existence in England. He is determined to gather the new sensations in England for his self-discovery. Krishan shows his full faith in Iqbal s mysticism when he says:

> So to exist is to be. And to be is to become aware. Matter cannot become. Every new experience makes me. I can choose to be. Nature cannot. I have the freedom of choice. I can create myself through my consciousness.[18]

Anand records in his masterpiece *The Bubble* various events and situations, which help his characters, undergo the process of self-discovery. The self in contemporary society is fragmentary. Krishan tries to find his hidden selves through expiation and re-examination. He is able to achieve some kind of a structured whole. His ability to find larger frames of meaning gives his sense of significance as an individual. He does not lose his grip on life because he does not lack the structure of meaning. He does experience boredom and depression, but they do not weaken his will to live. Man is a teleological animal and his pure survival does satisfy his need for significance. Krishan is full of despair when Prof. Dicks dismisses India as a mumbo-jumbo. He remembers gratefully the phrases of Dayal Singh to counter the feeling of Prof. Dicks:

> Man is on a journey to the unknown sun. But he has no shelter. He seems uprooted. He has to find a home in ecstasy.[19]

Krishan does not appreciate Gautam s stress on the effacement of the self and his Nirwana is, for Krishan, the state of nothingness. Love, hate, adversity and death are the facts of existence and they have much to do with the evolutionary process of life. Krishan writes in his letter to his friend, Noor:

> The wish to move forward filled me with a warmth, that urged me on. I wanted to live, to breathe, to expand my soul, to run wild.[20]

Krishan s encounter with women paves the path to his progress. Women bring a transformation in his character. Evelyn reveals the platonic aspect of love, whereas Lucy symbolizes innocence and purity. She is part of negation and emptiness symbolized by Buddha whose philosophy is for Anand bereft of drama and magic. It s Irene who like Clara gives Krishan the desired ecstasy and fulfilment. Irene liberates him from all the fear and terror into an ocean of light. He feels lighter when there is a physical union between the two. Yashmin had given his some warm glimmering and her frail body gives him despair while the changing hues and the varying moods of Irene s face give him the joy of self-discovery. Life, for Krishan, is not only the rhythmic flow of nerves but also the renewal of vibrations within. Anand may be criticized for emphasizing much on body in *The Bubble*. But he does not like to call body a prison house and an isolated lump of flesh and bone. The body is a living link with the world and it is more a liberator than a fetter. If love is an outflow of surplus energy it has something to do with the self of the vital needs of the body. Krishan shows that a life of ideal harmony is not possible without an awareness of the body. It is body, which gives him the sense of his identity and harmony with the universe. This creates in him the feeling of wholeness.

Anand s women characters, too, share the equal identity crisis. They are soft, sober, suppressed and subjected to persecution yet they are sublime. It s in *The Old Woman or The Cow* that we find Gouri struggling against all odds to secure her identity. Her silent suffering climaxes into the delightful moment of her complete liberation. She slams the door against her husband and explodes the old myth of the suffering and enduring Sita devoured by the earth. Gouri s life is a pilgrimage of hope and faith. Her inner transformation is a moment of triumph that gives no delight. She is not like Noor who succumbs to despair. She organizes her emotions to bring substance and significance. She does not allow her cultural conditioning to deform her into an image of self-surrender and despair. Likewise, Gangu s daughter, Leila in *Two Leaves* radiates with a new light. Anand shows his greater admiration for women in general and Gangu s wife in particular when he says:

> There is something of water about a woman. Flowing, always flowing one way or another; restless like the waves, sometimes overwhelmingly moody fickle and capricious as a river in a storm, sometimes bright and smiling, sometimes soft and sad but always tender and kind.[21]

Thus we find that the individual s search for identity is the central preoccupation of Anand in most of his novels. To A.V. Krishna Rao, this is a stage of synthesis in which the private and the public components of life are integrated. The loss of identity in his novels is a moment of despair for the hero but when he regains his identity after a prolonged struggle, it is a moment of delight for him. The fact that Anand s hero is not without grit and guts gives the readers delight. The quest theme which is found in every novel has its share of despair and delight. Anand s hero in each novel grows and becomes progressively more sure of himself passing from a low level of consciousness to a more happy adulthood. The turbulent moment born out of his encounter with other points of view is a creative crisis full of despair and delight. The critical juncture in each novel tests resources and resilience of the hero. The fact that the opposing images of the individual and society are fused, emphasizes the primacy of delight. The evolution of a new self for each hero through strain and tension towards hope and fulfilment is a familiar pattern.

Anand believes that man can emerge from the breakdown, the disruption and the decay. Poverty and hunger inspire courage. Man can contend with the disruptive forces and can conquer them. If there s discord in life it is a stage and not a terminus. Life is a pattern of despair and delight and it is not without its dynamic thrust. Man has to make and re-make himself for an authentic living. The nightmare of living in a hostile world brings fear and disquiet for men but the solitary contemplative sinks again into the quiet of self-communion. Man has in him not only the noises of the earth but also the silence of the seas and music of the year. Anand s characters suffer the crisis of identity no doubt, but on regaining their identity after a prolonged struggle it is a moment of delight for them. Radhakrishnan, too, endorses what the protagonist of Anand s novel does:

> For the flower to develop the bud has to die, for the fruit the flower, for the seed the plant and for the plant the seed. Life is a process of eternal birth and death. All progress is sacrifice.[22]

NOTES AND REFERENCES

1. M.R. Anand, The Story of My Experiments with a white lie, in *Critical Essays* ed. M.K. Naik, 16.
2. M.R. Anand, *Untouchable*, 57.
3. *Ibid.*, 55.

4. Dieter Reimenschneider, Alienation in the novels of Anand , in *Perspective,* ed. by K.K. Sharma, 96.
5. M.R. Anand, *Untouchable,* 97.
6. M.R. Anand, *Coolie,* 318.
7. M.R. Anand, *Two Leaves and a Bud,* 146.
8. R. Shepherd, Alienated Being in *Perspectives,* 143.
9. M.R. Anand, *The Village,* 229.
10. M.R. Anand, *The Big Heart,* 68.
11. *Ibid.,* 17.
12. M.R. Anand, *Death of a Hero.*
13. M.R. Anand, *The Private Life.*
14. P.K. Rajan, *Studies in M.R. Anand,* 95.
15. M.R. Anand, *Seven Summers,* 23.
16. M.R. Anand, *Morning Face,* 438.
17. M.R. Anand, *Confession of a Lover,* 160.
18. M.R. Anand, *The Bubble,* 72.
19. *Ibid.,* 18.
20. *Ibid.,* 81.
21. M.R. Anand, *Two Leaves,* 148.
22. M.R. Anand, *Preface to Apology for Heroism,* 99.

4

Indian Nuances of Anand s English: An Examination of His Early Novels

ASHOK KUMAR BACHCHAN

Mulk Raj Anand adopts English as the medium of his artistic expression and nourishes it to proper growth, in his own way. He applies various methods, techniques and devices to impart an Indian identity to his English as an untiring experimenter. T.D. Brunton reflects on the tendencies and possibilities of the Indianization of English:

> When a novel first reached India in the late 18th and 19th century, it must have seemed quite strange, even to those few educated Indians who could read English [...]. The strength and maturity of much Indian writing in English are beyond dispute, and it ought not to be necessary at this stage to ask such questions whether an Indian can write in English. But amidst much bold creativity, there still lingers a sterile tradition which blights even major talents [...]. The tradition I refer to is that of Indianness. It is still frequently assumed that a novel in English by an Indian author can only be justified if it is Indian in some peculiar and essential fashion. Thus novels come to be valued not so much upon their power as fiction, as upon their content of this national quintessence.[1]

There are many reasons for justifying the peculiarities of Indo-English novels *viz.* peculiar Indian speech-habits, social conditions, traditional values, ethical and theological concepts which distinguish and identify Indian life. At a moment of sudden pain an Indian (except the Christians who live here) never cries Christ, O, Christ! but Ram, He Ram or Ya Allah or Wahe Guru , etc. There would be nothing more absurd than to depict Indian peasants, labours and outcastes in the standard British diction and phraseology. In Anand s pre-Independence novels, *i.e.* the novels of the first phase, characters with all their social, personal, economic, political and religious problems and linguistic habits seem to be moving and breathing with us. He wrote *Untouchable* (1935), *Coolie* (1936), *Two Leaves and a Bud* (1937), *The Village* (1938), *Across the Black Waters* (1938) and *The Sword and the Sickle* (1940). The last novel of this phase is *The Big Heart* (1945). He is so alive to Indian consciousness, Indian sensibility and to the problem of exploitation of the poor by the rich that the entire locale of Indian life is recreated before the reader.

Dr M.R. Anand s characters grow on the Indian soil and imbibe the Indian culture in all its rusticity as well as refinement. We may for convenience categorise Anand s use of Indianism in the following groups: (i) Use of popular Indian idioms and phrases, (ii) Indian terms of abuse, expletives, swear-words, distorted Indian words and sentences, and distorted English words, (iii) Indian imagery, symbols, similes and metaphors, (iv) Dialogues transliterated from the vernacular and (v) Reflection of the social, political, religious, moral and cultural aspects of Indian life.

POPULAR INDIAN IDIOMS AND PHRASES

Dr Anand uses a number of transliterated Indian idioms and phrases in his early novels in order to impart an Indian flavour to his English. These idioms and phrases catch the rhythm and tone of the vernacular speech most of the time. They also match with Indian culture and Indian sensibility which distinguish Indian English from American, Australian or African English. For example, most of the invocational phrases mentioned below are chanted by Indians, either at moments of excitement or while they take bath or when they go to bed at night or get up in the morning:

(a) *Ram, Ram Sri, Hari Narayan; Sri Krishna* (*U.* 65),[2] (b) *Hey Hanuman Jodha* (*U.* 65), (c) *Om, Shanti Deva* (*U.* 65), (d) *Kali Mai* (*U.* 65), (e) *Arti, Arti* (*U.* 68), (f) *Sri Ram Chandra Ki Jai* (*U.* 68), (g) *Alakh, Alakh* (*U.* 80), (h) *Bham Bham Bhole*

Nath (*U.* 80), (i) *Krishnaji Maharaja* (*U.* 155), (j) *Jai Deva* (*U.* 35), (k) *Ya Allah* (*U.* 196), (1) *Ishwar, Ishwar Parmeshwar* (*TLB.* 84). It is supposed that the various names of gods and goddesses may relieve one of cares and anxieties and bring peace and prosperity. *Mahatma Gandhi ki jai* (*U.* 151), *Hindu Mussulman ki jai* and *Mahatma Gandhi ki jai, Harijan ki jai* (*U.* 167), *Mahatmaji ki jai* (*U.* 167) were some popular slogans during the Freedom struggle in India.

There are some peculiarly Indian ji formations to depict a formal respect, such as *Punditji* (*U.* 32), *babuji* (*U.* 90), *mianji* (*U.* 48), *Sadhuji* (*U.* 80), *Mahatmaji* (*U.* 157), *Krishnaji* (*U.* 155), *Bhaiji* (*U.* 156), *Yogiji* (*C.* 155), *Havildarji* (*U.* 18), *Lallaji* (*C.* 35), *Hakimji* (*U.* 90). These interjections impart a special Indian colour to Anand s language.

A number of Indian phrases are used to describe Indian characters, situations, beliefs and are not very different from their counterparts in the vernacular. They function differently, sometimes as common invocations or address and sometimes as noun, adjective, verb or adverb. They also throw light on Indian customs and manners, and sometimes they become symbolic of their poverty: *mud-walled houses* (*U.* 11), *leather-worker□s son* (*U.* 12), *egg-shaped face* (*U.* 43), *low-caste boys* (*U.* 45), *henna-dyed beards* (*U.* 47), *betel-leaf shop* (*U.* 47), *remnant seller□s stall* (*U.* 63), *maize-flour bread* (*U.* 86), *a little breath-left* (*U.* 91), *tailor-master□s son* (*U.* 126), *bandmaster□s sons* (*U.* 126), *become a nawab* (*U.* 131), *turned-up moustache* (*U.* 136), *cast off trousers* (*U.* 146), *smoke-scented evening* (*U.* 160), *grass-cutter□s wife* (*U.* 146), *Angrezi Sarkar* (*TLB.* 3), *two-horned yama* (*TLB.* 3), *Ram, Ram brother* (*TLB.* 36), *no consideration for anyone□s mother or sister* (*TLB.* 42), *Salaam Huzoor* (*TLB.* 49), *cow-dung cakes* (*TLB.* 76), *lifting joined hands* (*TLB.* 148), *open-air kitchen* (*TLB.* 152), *The Congress wallahs* (*TLB.* 212), *a springtime of her beauty* (*TLB.* 214), *Hai Ma Hai* (*TLB.* 259), *gazelle-eyed courtesans* (*TLB.* 264), *burning with fever* (*TLB.* 79), *La hol billah!* (*TBH.* 78), *wah Guru!* (*TBH.* 26), *the cow-dust hour* (*TBH.* 172), *eyed the young girls* (*TV.* 55), *to be a lion□s son* (*TV.* 221), *deeds worthy of forefathers* (*TV.* 222), *struck by the hand of fate* (*ATBW.* 197), *talking openly to girls* (*ATBW.* 84), *the sepoy heart* (*ATBW.* 231), *grovel in the dust with joined hands* and *the mainspring of convention* (*TV.* 223).

Thakur Guru Prasad[3] takes no notice of the above mentioned phrases which help in presenting intimately the various aspects of Indian life in a language approximated to the vernacular. They not only impart special Indian flavour to Anand s English but also gives English its Indian domicile. There are some typical Indian forms of address such as: *the mother of my daughter; the mother of Leila; Ram, Ram brother,* etc. In the conservative Indian society, a person does not mention the name of his wife; so he addresses her as mother of someone (name of his son or daughter).

The following determiners have been borrowed from regional languages: *leather-worker□s son, egg-shaped face, low-caste boys, high class men, tailor-master□s son* and *grass-cutter□s wife.* We encounter some such phrases as are rendered from Punjabi or Hindustani expressions: *a little breath left, become a nawab, Angrezi Sarkar* (British government), *the Congress wallahs* (the members of the Congress party), *a springtime of* [...] *beauty* (age of charming youth), *cry* [...] *eyes out* (weep bitterly), *the cow-dust hour* (twilight), *the owner of my house* (husband), *to be a lion□s son* (to be brave), *deeds worthy of forefathers* (noble deeds), *talking openly to girls* (to be shameless in Indian context) and *the sepoy heart* (hard heart).

Indian ways or manners of obeisance are indicated by such phrases as *lifting joined hands, raised hands to forehead* and *grovel in the dust with joined hands.* These phrases show how poor people from low-castes paid respects to socially superior beings.

There are some idioms, proverbs and superstitions which have been transliterated from the original Punjabi, Hindi and Urdu languages to create an Indian atmosphere or to suggest the Indian background of the concerned characters such as: (a) *to teach* [...] *the lesson* (*U.* 109), (b) *A straw in the beard of a thief* (*U.* 117), *guilty conscience,* (c) *Gold teeth in the mouth of a thief* (*U.* 117), *prosperity of an evil-doer,* (d) *not see* [...] *face again* (*U.* 132, excessive hatred), (e) *Mouth watered* (*U.* 86, an intense gustatory sensuousness), (f) *Men with abiding purpose cherish neither hatred nor love* (*TLB.* 173), (g) *to eat ashes* (*TBH.* 122, to suffer), (h) *A single plea will not burst the oven!* (*TBH.* 116, a single person cannot change the order of life), (i) *Even the loin-cloth of a running thief is good enough* (*TBH*. 118, something is better than nothing), (j) *the chicken at home is equal to lentils* (*THB*. 91, devaluating a familiar thing or familiarity breeds contempt), (k) *iron cuts iron* (*TBH*. 147, like cures like), (l) *a well-fed man needs religion* (*TBH*. 155), (m) *A crow tried to strut like a peacock* (*TBH*. 168), (n) *What can a dog know of the taste of butter* (*TBH*. 199), (o) *running with the hare and hunting with the hounds* (*TBH*. 202, hypocrite), (p) *The camels are being swept away, the ants say they float* (*TBH*. 211), (q) *Never believe a barber or a brahmin* (*TLB*. 8), (r) *Warm the hand* (*TLB*. 111, to bribe), (s) *If wishes could rain, cowherds would be kings* (*TLB*. 169), (t) *to bring a piece of iron home on Monday was the sure harbinger of an impending tragedy* (*TLB*. 116, superstition), (u) *If the frog makes water on your hand, you will get leprosy* (*TLB*. 110, superstition), (v) *throw away the turban off* [...] *head* (*C* 252, disparaging act), (w) *Cut nose* (*TV*. 39, to insult) and (x) *to cut the throat of* (*ATBW*. 246, to slay). The idioms, phrases and proverbs mentioned above are functional and not a useless embellishment of the language by Anand. They reveal characters and situations and also catch the spirit of Indian life.

INDIAN TERMS OF ABUSE, EXPLETIVES, SWEAR-WORDS, DISTORTED INDIAN AS WELL AS ENGLISH WORDS AND SENTENCES

Anand s novels are littered with terms of abuse, expletives or curses, swear-words and with so many Indian and English words and sentences in their distorted form. The dialect of central Punjab which influences Anand s English so much and which is the mother-tongue of many of his characters is full of such expressions. They reveal the nature, the status and the social condition of the characters who use them. Commonly, the illiterate, unsophisticated and peevish characters abundantly use these items of Indianism. The following catalogue contains:

(a) Terms of Abuse

Lover of your mother (*U*. 12), *Son of a pig* (*U*. 15), *betichod* (*TBH*. 180), *Bitch! Prostitute wanton* (*U*. 28), *Eater of dung and drinker of urine* (*U*. 29), *You swine* (*U*. 53), *Cock-eyed son of a bow-legged scorpion!* (*U.* 53), *Dirty dog! son of a bitch! offspring of a pig* (*U.* 53), *son of a dog!* (*U.* 55), *vay, eater of your masters, may the vessel of your lie never float in the sea of existence, may you perish and die (U.* 80), *O bey brother-in-law* (*U.* 102), *oh, illegally begotten* (*U.* 102), *shut up bitch* (*U.* 103), *The wife of a hundred husbands* (*TLB.* 168), *the daughter of a shameless mother* (*TLB.* 168), *Owls!* (*TBH.* 39), *Rape mothers!* (*TBH.* 214), *rape-sister* (*TBH.* 214), *the bitch goddess machine!* (*TBH.* 216), *vultures* (*TBH.* 227), *bahinchod!* (*C.* 200).

The most remarkable point about these expletives and abuses is that their number decreases from novel to novel. As Anand gains in maturity and experience, he avoids using them or confines them to a very limited number. But whenever they are used, they are never out of the context. People from Punjab it is a fact get up with them, live for the whole day with them and also go to bed with them.

(b) Indian words and phrases and Indianized English words or distorted English expressions

Untouchable. *Jemadar* (14), *goras* (12), *Baksheesh* (15), *Sahib* (14), *bania* (23), *izzat* (15), *maidan* (24), *Hai Hai* (29), *Pundit* (30), *jalebis* (31), *kheer* (31), *kara parshad* (31), *Han* (34), *Acha* (40), *Puff-puffing* (36, onomatopoeia), *burra babu* (42), *Tan-Nana-Nan Tan* (47, onomatopoeia), *biris* (47), *bazaar* (49), *rasgulas, gulabjamans* and *ladus* (51, Indian sweetmeats), *Lat sahib* (55), *Laften Gornor* (55), *Kalijug* (55), *Nahin* (55), *langar* (98), *chapatis* (86), *Hakim* (90), *dawaikhana* (90), *dakdar* (90), *Bhangi* (92, sweeper), *chandal* (92), *sarkar* (92), *tamasha* (69, show), *ghats* (99), *handi* (93), *yar* (109), *sahibhood* (113), *Mehrbani* (120), *Nawab* (131), *jao* (138), *chamars* (147), *girja ghar* (142), *avtar* (153), *Dilli* (154), *Kothi* (154, edifice), *vilayat* (154), *swadharma* (155), *Sarkari Adalat* (156), *panchayat* (156, local court), *puggareed* (160, with puggaree on head), *pandal* (160), *ksatriya, vaishya, sudras* (164), *swadeshi* (168), *maya* (170, illusion), *nirvana* (170, redemption), *Nawan jug* (272, New or Naween becomes Nawan in Punjabi), *Karma* (172), *oh Maharaj! Maharaj* (130), *Salaam babuji* (42), *twice-born* (19), *kala admi zamin par hangne wala* (21-22), *I have only one life to live* (51), *Don't know what the world is coming to* (54), *You sweepers have lifted your head to the sky nowadays* (81), *Is this* *your father□s house that you come and rest here?* (80), *Tum udas* (137), *Sur ka bacha* (139), *Kute ka bacha* (139), *Ither Ither!* (147), *mem sahib* (148, English woman), *take a ploughman from the plough, wash off his dirt,* and *he is fit to rule a kingdom* (172), *Salad* (95) and *The Babu□s sons were babu□s sons* (125).

Two Leaves and a Bud. *Seth* (3), *Chowkidar* (3, guard), *mai bap* (4), *Parbat* (11), *Sayce* (33), *Pukka kothi* (34, brick-built edifice), *angrezi log* (34), *basti* (34, village), *Kismet* (37, luck), *budmash* (42, stupid), *bacho* (47, save yourself), *Gurkha* (49), *Mistri* (58), *the khansamah* (53), *Shaitan* (65, Devil), *Ping-Pong* (a Punjabi game, 94), *darji* (94, tailor), *swargbash* (107, death), *daftar* (109, office), *motucar* (111, motor-car), *chaprasi* (111, peon), *nazrana* (111, gift), *Hum hum Ho Hum* (145), *Purdah* (148, curtain), *dai* (171, midwife), *charpai* (166, cot), *thup* (154, *dhup* or incense becomes thub in Punjabi), *Ashshtant* (171, assistant), *Sabha* (210, meeting), *Fakir* (210), *Railgaries* (211), *Zoolm* (213), *Zalim* (214, tyrant), *a ginn or a bhut* (246, evil spirits), *Shikaries* (252, hunters), *Kheddah* (252, trap for elephants), *dhotied* (268, wearing dhoti), *Flat-nosed gurkha woman* (51), *Acha hai* (56), *Koi hai* (60), *pahlwan* (62, wrestler), *gymkhana* (61), *Ja! Ja! chala ja* (115), *Hosh karo* (193, come to senses), *By the oath of God* (197, by God), *Khabardar! Chalo! Jao!* (206, Be warned, go away), *Satis* (57, women burnt on the pyre of their husbands).

The Big Heart. *goonda* (173), *kalal khana* (119, ale house), *ohe buk nahin, bastard* (209), *ohe chup kar!* (111, be silent), *That is the true talk* (191, that s the matter), *Hut duray, duray* (145), *puris* (54, loaves fried in ghee), *Injan* (59, Engine), *dacoos* (155), *hookah* (172), *Bombai* (173, Bombay), *Maulvis and Pundits* (210), *Coal-black face* (20), *remorseless wheel of Jagannath* (88), *I wish I could take your fever myself* (175), *I beg you stop this kind of talk, ohe brothers* (210), *oh putar* (109, oh son).

Coolie. *Mochi* (299, cobbler), *May be live child* (152), *tortoise speed* (154), *langotis* (238, loin-clothes), *Jaldi chalo* (211, Hurry up).

Anand uses these very words, idioms, phrases, proverbs, expletives, swear-words, Anglicized Hindi, Urdu or Punjabi sentences, words and epithets over and over again in his novels. They become familiar not only to the Indian readers but also to the readers abroad. The number of these items decreases by and by in successive novels. As enumerated, there are only rare examples of distorted English words such as *fashun, motucar* and *injan* as they are as naturally used by the Indian speakers of the rank of Rakha, Lakha, Gulabo, Narayan, Ralia and many like them, as an Englishman uses Hindi words like *Coi hai, tum udas, kute ka bacha,* etc. Therefore, Meenakshi Mukherjee s[4] objection to their use does not carry conviction.

INDIAN IMAGERY, SYMBOLS, SIMILES AND METAPHORS

Mulk Raj Anand makes use of Indian images, symbols, similes and metaphors which have a definite bearing upon the social, cultural, religious and situational facts of Indian life such as (a) steaming earthen saucepan, tumblerful of tea (*U.* 16, symbol of stark poverty), (b) sacred thread twisted around their left ear (*U.* 20, a religious rite of the Brahmins), (c) brahminee bull (*U.* 60, an ox is offered in the memory of someone dead in India), (d) beating their breasts in mourning for the dead (*U.* 77), (e) Smoke-bottomed handi (*U.* 93, symbolizes poverty of the person who uses it), (f) a tall girl with a face as brown as ripe wheat and hair as black as the rain clouds (*U.* 97, simile for describing a beautiful girl), (g) Baba pese de (*U.* 150, a slogan of Indian beggars), (h) fierce-looking red-cheeked Pathans (*U.* 152), (i) clean-shaven head (*U.* 159, Indian sanyasis do shave their heads and sometimes Hindus get their heads shaved as a symbol of mourning for a dead relative), (j) two-bricks with-a-space-in between fireplace (*U.* 16, showing poverty of the outcastes), (k) The betel-leaf seller threw some water over it (nicked coin given by Bakha) [...]. Then he flung a red-lamp cigarette at Bakha, as a butcher might throw a bone to an insistent dog sniffing round the corner of his shop (*U.* 48, an image of humiliation of the low castes), (l) The swarms of crows, which blackened the sky like the harbingers of famine and which are now spreading over the countryside with droves of vultures around them, spell the surest disaster (*TBH.* 18, an ominous symbol of destruction), (m) And he could hear the dead mourning under the feet of the woman, whom he soon recognized as the goddess Kali, for her tongue was bulging out red, and her eyes were like two sharp glint discs shining like diamonds from the coal-black face (*TBH,* an image of Kali, a symbol of destruction for the devils), (n) suspended by the tuft-knot over the edge of the burning ground in the hands of Yama (*TBH.* 38, Yama is the symbol of death), (o) Oh, he was such a noble creature much nobler than all those lotus! (*TBH.* 227, Lotus is a simile of beauty and grandeur), (p) O God, Let the earth open up and swallow me! otherwise they will destroy me, the vultures who are sitting (*TBH.* 227, Janki refers here to Sita who was swallowed up by the earth after being abandoned by Lord Rama. It is a typical mythological Indian symbol), (q) Come ni, Leila, come vay, Budhu (*TBH.* 35, ni and vay are specially Punjabi forms of address or suffix to effect Punjabi tone), (r) A distance of three days and three nights (*TLB.* 36, an Indian way of expressing distance), (s) eyes like long beans, great big noses like fried dumplings [...] twisted faces bursting with skin diseases like rotten melons (*TBH.* 66, Indian similes), (t) come and buy, come and buy! (*TBH.* 70, a slogan of stall keepers in a fair to attract the buyers), (u) he stepped back without showing his posterior (*TLB.* 133, an Indian court manner observed in Mughal darbars), (v) what can we do, Huzoor? You are our mai-bap, Huzoor (*TLB.* 200, a faithful presentation of low-caste people), (w) I fall at your feet (*TV.* 55, a Punjabi way of greeting an elder), (x) they were struck by the hand of Fate (*ATBW.* 197, an Indian way of expression for people with ill-luck), (y) Behold, the brother-in-law thought to take his hand to his head and salaamed the Germans [...] he abused the Angrez sahibs and made a sign as if he meant to cut the throat of the whole Angrezi race (*ATBW.* 246), (z) backboneless creatures who would abjectly catch hold of the feet of a policeman and grovel in the dust with joined hands [...] (*TSTS.* 279, a symbolical picture of the humility of the low-caste people).

DIALOGUES TRANSLITERATED FROM THE VERNACULAR (PUNJABI, HINDI OR URDU)

Dr Anand transliterates many Punjabi, Urdu and Hindi clauses, sentences and expressions to make his dialogues appear natural and appropriate for the concerned characters. Very much like Charles Dickens and the Russian novelists, he reaches the core of his characters hearts and the inmost recesses of their minds and succeeds in giving voice to their thoughts, emotions and feelings. Anand s characters belong to the lower sections of Indian society and that in their day-to-day life they do not converse in English. Since they are illiterate, unsophisticated, they cannot speak even their own regional language correctly. They use many distorted English words and they are also made to use numerous words, idioms and phrases from their colloquial language in their transliterated forms. The dialogues of Anand s early novels may be divided into three categories:

(i) An illiterate rustic talking to another person of his or her class

Anand s novels of the first phase are literally crowded with illiterate characters. He wields their speech in such a way that not only their intonation but their joys and fears, agonies and rancour, love and hatred are properly voiced. The whole characteristics of the class of characters are reflected through their dialogues so much so that they appear natural and animated.

Bakha touches a Hindu by chance in the market and the latter hurls a torrent of abuses on the former in *Untouchable*:

> Dirty dog! son of a bitch! offspring of a pig! keep to the side of the road, the low caste vermin! why don t you call you swine and announce your approach! Do you know you have touched me and defiled me, cock-eyed son of a bow-legged scorpion! Now I will have to go and take a bath to purify myself. And it was a new dhoti and a shirt I put on this morning! (52-53)

The speaker s contempt towards a low-caste boy like Bakha is well recorded in this dialogue. It reveals the vulgarity of his language and his orthodoxy. Anand does not want to strain himself to Indianize the borrowed language; he rather wants to reflect an actual social condition in a touch and defile Indian society and succeeds in doing so.

In *Untouchable,* an illiterate housewife showers curses and abuses on Bakha who happens to sit on the wooden platform of her house to rest for a while in a colloquial Indian language rather than English:

> Vay, eater of your masters, may the vessel of your life never float in the sea of existence. May you perish and die! you have defiled my house! Go! Get up, get up! Eater of your masters! why don t you shout if you wanted food? Is this your father s house that you come and rest here. (80)

In *The Big Heart,* the characters like Murlidhar, Karmo Devi and Ralia use a similar language to express themselves. Karmo Devi beseeches her step-son, Ananta:

> Han, son, it is all for you; only for you. So don t be hard on your old mother. I have cried my eyes out for years waiting for your bride. You don t know what it will mean to me. The women of the brotherhood will come to beat the drum, and there will be the bridal party [...] oh then shall the Gods bless us and your bride will come home and fall at your feet. (26)

There are numerous such examples of phrases and expressions in *The Big Heart.*

In *Coolie,* we come across a series of dialogues spoken by illiterate people which have in them the element of vulgarity and distortion of the standard British English. Anand records the plight of exploited coolies and the inhuman behaviour of the privileged-class people. Chimta Sahib, an illiterate foreman chides Hari who seeks re-employment in the former s factory:

> You think bloody fool, that you go away when you like and come back when you like and get the same pay all the time? The burra sahib has ordered me not to take any coolies back who have once left. He does not want old and used men. I am doing you a favour bahinchod. (199-200)

Piari Jan addresses Ratan, the wrestler in *Coolie*:

> Aao, welcome, Pahalwanji. Where have you kept yourself hidden so long? My eyes have gone blind looking at

> the way along which you were to come to grace my house. (214)

The above expression cannot be rendered in its true spirit in standard English. The Hindi word Aao translated into come and the expressions where have you kept yourself hidden so long and My eyes have gone blind [ ] to grace my house ; if changed a little, may distort Piari Jan s Indian character.

Gangu and Narayan, the two poor coolies at Macpherson Tea Estate in *Two Leaves and a Bud,* talk to each other:

> Ram, Ram brother said Narayan, an emaciated little man, as he came up with a hookah in his hand, bare except a loin-cloth.
>
> Ram, Ram said Gangu with a smile. Have you come from afar? asked Narayan, A distance of three days and three nights, said Gangu [...]. (112)

The address Ram, Ram brother and the expression A distance of three days and three nights convey the illiteracy of the persons conversing. That they are utterly poor is reflected through the images of hookah and loin-cloth.

(ii) An uneducated person talking to an educated or urban character

When an illiterate person talks to an educated person we discover utter humility and minimum distortion of the language in dialogues. Such characters as Sauda and Mohan in *Coolie,* Ananta, Puran Singh and Janki in *The Big Heart* are more or less educated and therefore use a sophisticated language with only a few colloquial expressions. We rarely come across the terms of abuse, swear-words or curses in them. Sauda incites coolies against the tyranny of the owners of the factory:

> You are human beings. Have you forgotten your notion of izzat? Would you let anyone throw the turbans off your head? (252)

The hybrid term notion of izzat and the expression throw away the turbans off your head reveal the Indian identity of the speaker. He seems to be talking in a colloquial language.

Puran Singh Bhagat in *The Big Heart* speaks a language similar to that used by the characters of R.K. Narayan. He proves to be a true mouthpiece of Anand through his following utterance:

> All the world is in a whirl in which men and women are devastating each other, while delirium burns the cities and villages of *Hindustan*. I tell you there is hope for our land except in Revolution. But that requires devotion and thought. Perhaps it will be achieved through *Uncle Viroo s belief in Karma*; if not by reciting the verses of Karma. Sow good seeds and you will reap good deeds only I believe you get your reward here on earth and not in heaven. (62)

Anand s English characters are shown anglicizing Indian sentences and words. Reggie Hunt, the worst exploiter of the poor coolies on Macpherson Tea Estate addresses the revolting coolies:

> Hosh Karo! Hosh Karo! Have you no sense! Donkeys? [...] I will shoot you all, Reggie roared [...]. Because, Sahib none of our wives, sisters and mothers are safe, someonc vcntured from the back of the crowd.
>
> Dare you utter a sound and I will shoot you dead, he snarled. (193-94)

(iii) An educated person conversing with educated persons

Dialogues among educated persons, though rare in the novels of the first phase, are less racy and impressive because we find the rhythm of vernacular speech missing in them. Images, life-styles of speakers, and the specific references bear testimony to the Indian background of these dialogues. The dialogues delivered by the poet and Mahatma Gandhi in *Untouchable*, by the Count in *The Sword and the Sickle*, the conversation between Ananta and his beloved, Janki, in *The Big Heart*, and the talk between Comrade Joshi and Lala Murlidhar in the same novel are good examples of such dialogues. Lala Murlidhar neglects his clan out of pride and later on he has to placate them by all means. He asks forgiveness from his clan:

> Listen brothers, I have put my turban at the feet of all of you, save this ceremony. *I have sinned*. I have erred. You can beat my old head with your shoes. But let us have this betrothal [...]. *A crow tried to strut like a peacock*

> but seeing his feet wept and cried. That is my condition. Forgive me. (162)

Anand wants to introduce Indian rites and rituals, ceremonies and customs and at the same time wins the curiosity of the readers both Indian and foreign. Therefore, it is natural that dialogues of educated characters in these novels are less impressive than those of the illiterate and rustic ones.

(iv) Reflection of the social, political, religious, moral and cultural aspect of Indian life.

Anand considers art as a means to some end in itself. As a true reformist-humanist, he wants to bring about a radical change in society, individuals and in politics. He challenges the century-old conventions and religious orthodoxy which hamper all the prospects of social, economic, mental and spiritual development of Indian people.

All the novels of the first phase were written during the pre-Independence period, and their central themes are pivoted around social evils such as untouchability, women s oppression, exploitation of children and labourers. There is only a feeble echo of independence movement in these novels.

In *Untouchable,* Anand s sympathy is fully reserved for the excommunicated section of society. In order to convince the reader that he is telling the story of India, Anand introduces so many references to Indian myths, puranas, history and characters in his novels. He finds likeness between Charat Singh who has a number of scars on his body and who always stands leaning by the goalpost and the character of the great Rajput warrior, Rana Sanga, the conqueror of Akbar, the great Mughal. [5]

Coolie, in fact, is an elaborated metaphor of unequal distribution of social, political and economic rights and resources among the Indian people. Daulatpur grain market provides a picture of an Indian market stuffed with filth, rubbish, dirt and deadly reeking remnants and Munoo wanders with Tulsi to earn something to help his kind master, Prabha Dayal. Even in such a polluted atmosphere of the market, the coolie remembers the name of God. Anand mocks at the religious blindness of Indian people who all the time chant the name of God in vain. Munoo bearing the son and daughter of Hari on his shoulder, reminds the novelist of the power-god, Hanuman. This reference seems to be wrong because in *The Ramayana* it is described that Lord Rama was offered a Pushpak viman by the god of wealth, Kuber to come from Ceylon to Oudh. At another point in the great epic, Hanuman carries the two brothers, Ram and Laxman on his shoulders from the demon king Ahiravana s prison-house.

Anand shows his earnest concern with the economic and political slavery of the poor coolies and labourers. One of them, Mohan, thus incites his fellowmen to rise against tyranny and oppression. Charles Croft Crooke s hatred for coolies in *Two Leaves and a Bud* is in its lowest form where he says to De la Havre, You and your bloody coolies ought all to be shot dead against a wall. De la Havre holds not only the English people but also the Indians philosophy of poverty responsible for their pitiable condition. By making passing references to the characters of Indian history such as Jehangir, Nur Mahal and Shah Jehan, the novelist tries to assure the readers that he is narrating a tale related to India. The reference to the Indian God Indra, the king of heaven in Indian mythology, brings out the Indianness of description.

Anand s artistic vision encompasses all: Indian culture, customs, rituals, ethics and myths. In *The Big Heart* he chooses a few individuals to depict the conflict between the old conventions and the new modernity. He seems to have developed the power of getting into the inmost essence of a character and finding out the situations and emotions which moulded them. There are many symbols, images and pictures from Indian myths or even local myths in *The Big Heart.* The philosophy of Lord Buddha (62), references to the Mahabharat war (67), Gautam Buddha (66), Jallianwala Bagh massacre (67), Maharaja Ranjit Singh (86), Rani Jindan (86), the remorseless wheel of Jagannath (88), Bombay strike of 1939 (88), Arya Samajis and Gandhiji all indicate the Indian background of *The Big Heart.*

The double standards of morality of the old Punjabi peasants is criticized by Lal Singh in *The Village.* He thus assails the practice of keeping Katch, Kara, Kirpan, Kesh and

Kanga followed by the conservative Sikhs even today. *Across the Black Waters* begins with Lal Singh s escape from his village and ends with his becoming a prisoner of war in Germany. In this war novel, the hero has to give up his obsessional assumptions about his country s glory. By observing the fashionable European girls he comes to realize Indian women s negligence about themselves. *The Sword and the Sickle* is also sprinkled with images, symbols, references and rituals drawn from Indian bucolic life.

Anand s linguistic experimentations in the first phase of his career are undeniably carried out for the purpose of art as well as for the expression of fictional reality.

NOTES AND REFERENCES

1. Brunton, T.D., India in Fiction: The Heritage of Indianness , *Critical Essays on Indian Writing in English,* (ed.) M.K. Naik, S.K. Desai, G.S. Amur (Dharwar, 1972), 200.
2. *U* in the brackets stands for *Untouchable* (Arnold Heinemann, 1984) and the digits indicate the page numbers. Similarly *TLB.* stands for *Two Leaves and a Bud* (Arnold Heinemann, 1983), *C* for *Coolie, TBH* for *The Big Heart, TV* for *The Village, ATBW* for *Across the Black Waters, TSTS* for *The Sword and the Sickle* and show the page numbers of the novels.
3. Thakur, Guru Prasad, *Experimentation with Language in Indian Writing in English,* (ed.) S.K. Desai (Kolhapur, 1974).
4. Mukherjee, Meenakshi, Beyond the Village, *Critical Essays on Indian Writing in English,* (Eds.) M.K. Naik, S.K. Desai, G.S. Amur (Dharwar, 1972).
5. Anand, M.R., *Untouchable* (A.H., 1984), 117.

5

Mulk Raj Anand's *Untouchable*: A Triumph of Narrative Skill

U.S. RUKHAIYAR

The narrative form of Mulk Raj Anand's novel *Untouchable* shows a skillful organization of the various tools of narration, *e.g.*, point of view, focus, atmosphere, characterization etc. as also imagery. The novel shows how the untouchable at the time the novel was written lived in inhuman conditions and were subjected to worst kinds of humiliation, sometimes on trifles and sometimes without any cause whatsoever. Two of the keynotes of the novel are pathos and irony, or better say, irony upon pathos. But, though the novel begins on a note of despair, it ends on a note of hope, with echoes from Shelley's ode to the *West Wind* and *Euganean Hills.*

Language is generally plain and simple. But, on occasions, there are images and symbols, some of them recurrent, charged with deep emotion. Sometimes words and phrases have subtle overtones. As we shall see, the book has been able to achieve an adequate narrative form.

We would do well to begin with what Mulk Raj Anand said about what he wanted to show in this novel:

> I wanted to bring to light the ghosts of the "dead souls" murdered without a rite by the Dharamabugs. I wanted to beckon all the phantoms, so that they should haunt the dreams of the half dead, and awaken them, may be, to the lingering sparks of life [...] I wanted to burn and shine like.
>
> Tiger, tiger, burning bright [...].[1]

Another passage in the same article may shed more light:

> The chance of reading of Arthur Rimbaud s *Season in Hell* verified my own preoccupation with the sympathetic journey through hell which, I felt, the outcastes had been going through, with little or no hope of heaven. I do not believe in the theory of Karma. So I tried to take over the poetic truth of Blake, the pictorial truth of Picasso s blue period, and Theodore Powy s fabulous manner, to compensate myself for the disbelief of Rimbaud. And as these influences penetrated into my self-discovery, all the miscellaneous strains fused into Bakha. The real cry was not recorded in the book, and held back deliberately, but the echo might be feared if anyone wants to listen: A man is a man and he is born equal to all other men. [2]

The narrator has used the third person point of view with all its three common devices, *viz.*, (1) omniscient point of view; (2) the intrusive narrator; and (3) the limited point of view.

At times there are internal monologues. Indianness is also there in both speech and atmosphere. Like *Ulysses,* this book deals with events of just one day.

The early pages show that the writer wants to draw our attention to two things first, how the sweepers lived in an inhuman condition; and, second, how, even after being a sweeper, Bakha has some rare human virtues *e.g.*, sincerity and efficiency; and urge for life; an urge to rise above his station. But Bakha was a child of modern India. The clear cut styles of European dress had impressed his naive mind. This stark simplicity had furrowed his old Indian consciousness and cut deep, new lines where all considerations which made India evolve a skirty costume as best fitted for the human body, lay domant. But Bakha looked at the Tommies, stared at with wonder and amazement. So he tried to copy them in every thing (13). This noted reappears with greater stress in another sequence:

> Bakha felt the keen urge of his sense of anticipation draw before his eyes the horrible prospects of all the future days of service in the town and the insults that

> would come with them [...]. And with this and other fashionable items of dress, he had built up a new world, which was his heaven, if for nothing else, because it represented a change from the old ossified order and the stagnant pools of the lane near which he was born. (87-88)

There is also a poet and singer in him. And he slowly, slipped into a song (20). My work will soon be finished, he said poetically (21). He feels that during the dreary hours of his work, he heard sweet music, which must have been inspired by his conscious fondness for Ram Charan s sister, who is now going to be married. During the day hours of his routine work at the latrines subsequently he had often heard the delicate strain of elfin music (98). We know music is the natural ally of love.

That is not the end of it. In the same sequence, Bakha is bearing the strong call of biological adulthood, a Lawrencian impulse. He gets a vision of embracing, squeezing and ravishing Ram Charan s sister. But, soon he realizes how sinful it was on his part to think so of a friend s sister (98-99). This shows a conflict between the natural and the moral.

He has respect for his person as well as for his nation. When the English person Col. Hutchinson wants to lure him to the Christian fold, he recoils, even though his own community has treated him so shabbily. Perhaps he knows the difference between the two kinds of servitude, and prefers the native to the alien.

The writer perhaps tries to underline the irony, the pity of situation that is, how a noble soul, an honest and efficient worker, and a lovable boy like Bakha has to face all kinds of insult and humiliation only because he is an untouchable.

The narrative presents some four to five incidents, all of which look like variations upon the same theme, *i.e.*, how the untouchables at that time were subjected to all kinds of humiliation sometimes on trifles and sometimes without any cause, perhaps, just for sadistic delight. Anand first narrates the incident and then records Bakha s reflections thereon.

The first is the touching-in-the-bazar incident. It was a custom at that time that when sweepers entered the town, they had to beat a drum hung around their waist to announce their approach so that those who did not want to get touched by them would be on guard. One day Bakha is in a jolly mood. He walks into the town. He buys some *jalebis* to eat. But as soon as he wants to eat them, a *Lalaji,* that is, a man of upper caste, gets touched by him as Bakha had forgot to announce his approach. This creates an ugly scene. The Lalaji begins to hurl at him abuse and rebuke. He calls him swine, dog (53). Dirty dog; son of bitch (*Ibid*) offspring of a pig (*Ibid*). Soon caste men gather there and begin to shower upon him abuse and humiliation. A shopkeeper, calls him rape sister (57). A child says baselessly that one day Bakha beat him. Bakha was surrounded by a barrier, not a physical barrier but a moral one (54).

The same image of barrier recurs in the Temple Scene:

> And yet there was a futility written on his face. He could not overstep the barriers which the conventions of his superiors had built up to protect their weakness against him. (73)

And further:

> There was an inseparable barrier between himself and the crowd, the barrier of caste. He was part of consciousness which he could share and yet not understand. He had been lifted from the gutter, through the barriers of space, to partake of a life which was his and yet not his [...]. (153)

The recollection looks like an internal monologue. Bakha feels:

> The cruel crowd, all of them abused abused, abused. Why are we always abused? The Sanitary inspector that always abused my father. They always abuse us. Because we are sweepers. Because we touch dung. They hate dung. I hate too. That s why I came here. I was tired of working in the latrines every day. That s why they don t touch us, the high castes. (58)

Another irony is that a Hindu humiliates a Hindu while a Muslim tanga-wallah is kind to him. He soothes Bakha and tells him to walk along:

> But he is a Muhammadan. They don't mind touching us, the Muhammadans and the Sahibs. It is only the Hindus, and the outcastes who are not sweepers. For him I am a sweeper, sweeper—untouchable! Untouchable! Untouchable! That's the word! Untouchable! Untouchable! I am an untouchable! (58-59)

It is to be noted that it may be one of the main grounds in the political equation in India today that the *dalits* feel closer to the Muslims than to the caste Hindus.

The repetition of the word untouchable about half a dozen times in quick spurts followed by the sign of exclamation, the jerking rhythm, very well delineates the agitation going on in the heart of Bakha at the moment.

Here, the author makes a fine use of irony upon pathos, "Like a ray of light shooting through the darkness, the recognition on his lot dawned upon him [...]." The use of light imagery in this context has a pungent irony. But Bakha is not a dead log like his father. He is very much alive. He does feel and react:

> But there was a smouldering rage in his soul. His feelings rise like spurts of smoke from a half smothered fire in fitful jerks when the recollection of abuse or rebuke he suffered kindled a spark in the ashes of remorse inside him. (57-58)

This image reminds us of the image of an 'unextinguished hearth/ashes and spark' in he last verse of Shelley's *West Wind.*

The same technique of action followed by Bakha's reaction to it is found in all the incidents.

Look at the Temple incident. The hypocritical priest Kali Nath calls Bakha's good-looking young sister Sohini to cleanse the temple toilets. But he molests her and makes evil suggestions. Sohini screams. Pandit Kali Nath, for fear of being found guilty, starts shouting that he has been defiled by Sohini.

Now, this scene deepens the irony of the earlier incident. If a sweeper touches a lalaji, he gets polluted. But a priest, a Brahmin, can touch an untouchable and that too for such a

Brahmin, can touch an untouchable and that too for such a purpose. But there is much more to this irony.

(1) In the hierarchy of Hindu caste system the Brahmins are supposed to be at the top, and they are revered by one and all. But here a Brahmin stoops so slow.

(2) What place has the Brahmin chosen to commit this unholy act? [...] A temple, the holiest place, the seat of God. What an irony!

(3) The caste men too take sides with him. They are not prepared even to listen to Sohini.

(4) Sohini gives a fair account of a modest Indian maid.

(5) Bakha fumes and gnashes to take revenge for the insult to his sister. But Sohini stops him from doing so because she feels that the caste men will jointly spring upon him and kill him.

The author s observation of Bakha s state of mind of the moment rings three notes: (1) the oppression by caste men; (2) Bakha s urge to retaliate; and (3) his helplessness. The novelist observes:

> A superb specimen of humanity he seemed whenever he made the high resolve to say something, to go and do something, his fine form rising like a tiger at bay. And yet there was a futility written on his face. He could not overstep the barriers which the conventions of his superiors had built up to protect their weakness against him. He could not invade the magic circle which protects a priest from attack by anybody, especially by a low-caste man? So, in the highest moment of his strength, the slave in him asserted itself, and he lapsed back, wild with torture, biting his lips, ruminating his grievances. (73)

The real irony lies in Bakha s high resolve to take revenge being thwarted by *futility* written on his face. Why? Because the caste men have erected barriers of convention to protect their excesses from being questioned. The writer conceives of Bakha as a tiger, but a tiger at bay.

Such comments by the author make the reaction of Bakha clearer and stronger.

The Hockey match incident sustains and develops the same note. When Bakha saves a small boy from being crushed in a stampede in a hockey match and takes him to his home, the child s mother, instead of thanking him for this admirable job, scolds him and says that it is he who must have been the root of the trouble.

That is to say, fault or no fault, the untouchables had to receive the abuse and rebuke of the caste men as daily food. The irony lies in this that Bakha gets rebuke where he should have got reward.

The Well incident shows how even for an essential thing like drinking water the untouchables had to wait for long hours at some public well for some kind caste men who could show mercy and pull for them water from the well. And even when the hypocritical priest Kali Nath does, so, it is inspired less by the service to the needy than by lust for the young women among them.

In the Sadhu incident, the housewife attends dotingly on a Sadhu. But when Bakha asks for a piece of bread, she gives it to him after long entreaty, and that too after seasoning it with abuse and rebuke. Now, anybody can guess who needs bread more the Sadhu or the Sweeper.

The same pattern is seen in the narration of minor events. But, with all this, the novel ends on a note of hope, and this suggestion comes three ways:

(1) Mahatma Gandhi himself appears in the novel and in course of his speech he observes:

> The fact that we address God as the purifier of the polluted souls makes it a sin to regard anyone born in Hinduism as polluted it is satanic to do so. (164)

(2) When people in large numbers are going to attend the meeting of Gandhiji, they feel that evil may end:

> It was as if the crowd had determined to crush everything, however, ancient or beautiful, that lay in the way of their achievement of all that Gandhi stood for. It was as if they knew by an instinct surer than conscious knowledge, that things of the decadence may be destroyed in order to make room for those of the

> new. It seemed as if, in trampling on the blades of green grass, they were deliberately, brutally trampling on a part of themselves, which they had begun to abhor and from which they wanted to escape to Gandhi. (152-53)

Again we get echoes from the first verse of Shelley s *West Wind:*

> Pestilence-stricken multitudes: O thou
> Who chariotest to their dark winty bed
> The winged seeds, where they lie cold and low
> Each like a corpse within its grave. (1.5-8)

This passage seems to be logical corollary of the passages dealing with oppression to the downtrodden. It looks like the irruption of the congregated might of the smouldering rage (58), tiger at bay (73) and a lion enmeshed in a net (105) and such other reactions taking the form of a volcano in the heart of Bakha and other *dalits.* This shows the narrative skill of the author. It sounds the destruction of the old order and the cherished construction of the new order. Perhaps that is why towards the end we find language becoming more metaphorical and symbolical anticipating an apocalypse.

(3) The last three pages (174-76) show a vision of dawn in a symbolic language:

> The fires of sunset were blazing on the distant horizon. As Bakha looked at the magnificent orb of terrible brightness glowing on the margin of the sky, he felt a burning sensation within him. (174)
>
> x x x
>
> The sun descended. The pale, the purple, the mauve of the horizon blended into darkest blue. A handful of stars throbbed in the heart of the sky. (175)

These lines recall the following lines of Shelley s *Euganan Hills:*

> Noon descends around me now:
> This the noon of autumn s glow,
> When a soft and purple mist
> Like a vapour amethyst
> Or an air-dissolved star

Mingling light and fragrance, far
From the curved horizon's bound
To the point of Haven's profound.
Fills the overflowing sky. (lines 255-93)

We may also mark the last two paragraphs of the book and the verbal overtones of some of their words and phrases:

> He (Bakha) emerged from the green of the garden into the slight haze of dust that rose from the road and the paths. As the brief Indian twilight came and went, a sudden impulse shot through the *transformation of the space and time,* and gathered all the elements that were dispersed in the stream of his soul into a tentative decision: I shall go and tell father all that Gandhi said about us' he whispered to himself, and what that clever poets said. Perhaps I can find the poet on the way and ask him about his machine. And he proceeded homewards. (175-76) (Emphasis added)

Anand has used some images and symbols recurrently, perhaps to stress the main notes. The most important image is one of fire, with its variants. Fire stands for, among other things, revolution and purification:

> Then he picked up a long poker and prodded the fire. Quickly it flared up, suddenly illuminating the furnace with its leaping red, gold and black flames, *an angry consuming power.* (23) (Emphasis added)

x x x

> The burning flame seemed to ally itself with him. It seemed to give him a *sense of power,* the power to destroy. It seemed to infuse into him a masterful instinct somewhat akin to sacrifice. It seemed as if *burning and destruction were for him acts of purification.* (24) (Emphasis added. The verbal overtones are too clear to be explained.)

When Bakha receives abuse and rebuke in the touching-in-the-bazaar incident:

> There was a smouldering rage in his soul. His feelings would rise like spurts of smoke from a half smothered fire in fitful jerks. (57-58)

After the Temple incident:

After the Temple incident:

> As he sauntered along a spark of some intuition suddenly set him ablaze. He was tired with a desire to burst out from the shadow of silence and obscurity in which he lay enshrouded. (106)

The last pages of the novel (174-76) show a different use of fire image. In the previous images fire suggests indignation, agitation and desire for revenge. But towards the end fire suggests the effulgent glow of a new dawn. It shows the post-resolutive phase, the light that comes out of a long process of struggle and suffering. It is the light that comes towards the end in *Macbeth.* It is the light of hope that comes after the darkness of suffering:

> The fires of sunset were blazing on the distant horizon. As Bakha looked at the magnificent orb of *terrible brightness* glowing on the margin of the sky, he felt a burning sensation within him. (174)

The following suggestions come out:

(1) The fire of sunset may suggest the burning of the decadent order.

(2) The phrase terrible brightness recalls Blake s Tiger, of which Anand felt enamoured in the passage quoted on page 1. On two occasions in the novel Bakha has been likened to a tiger once a tiger at bay (73), a lion enmeshed in a net (105). Just possible, Anand finds in him the Christ image. In the juvescence of the year Came Christ the tiger. (Eliot: *Gerontion*)

(3) That Bakha feels a burning sensation within him very well recalls the fire passages quoted above which suggest that he wished to burn the system but that he was helpless.

Now the hope is about to be fulfilled. And the subsequent passages give a vision of fulfilment The sun descended (175).

Similarly, the images of barrier, furrow, etc. also occur. Some of them appear in some of the passages quoted above.

On two occasions in the novel Anand has made a vitalist/ organicist use of language. When Havildar Charat Singh gives Bakha a brand new hockey stick, he is astonished:

> He was overcome by the man s kindness. He was grateful, grateful haltingly, grateful falteringly, grateful stumbling, grateful [...]. (122)

Similarly, the passage which describes Col. Hutchinson, uses so many polysyllabic and high-sounding words that we get an idea of the character of a hypocritical parson so well satirized by Chaucer and Langland:

> And he had swamped the overbearing strain of the upper middle class Englishman in him, by his hackneyed effusion of Christian sentiment camouflaged the narrow, insular patriotism of his character in the lingo of the white-livered humanitarian. (138)

This brief survey shows that in *Untouchable* Mulk Raj Anand has used not only a common, plain narrator s voice. When he describes a simple thing, he uses plain language. But when he describes an emotional sequence, he uses figurative language. He takes help of some powerful symbols and images. This device adds a poetic dimension to the novel. It seems he anticipated R.P. Blackmur s observation that if novel has to attain the stature of poetry or drama, it will have to cease to be mere chronicle and try to conform to the metaphoric structures. The narration is never dull, never flat. It is absorbing from the beginning to the end. The recurrence of the keynotes through plain narration as well as images and symbols reminds us of the methods used by Henry James, D.H. Lawrence and E.M. Forster. It is remarkable that Mulk Raj Anand made such a laudable attempt when Indian fiction in English was still its infancy. It must have served as a model for many of the subsequent practitioners of this art.

NOTE

All the textual passages have been cited from the book *Untouchable*, Arnold Publishers, New Delhi, Revised Edition, 1970.

REFERENCES

1. Anand, Mulk Raj, *The Story of My Experience with a Write lie*, Indian Literature Vol. 10, No. 3, 1967. Reprinted in *Critical Essays on Indian Writing in English*, Macmillan, Silver Jubilee Students Edition, 1977, 18.
2. *Ibid.* 17.

6

Humanistic Note: A Study in Mulk Raj Anand s *The Old Woman and the Cow*

RAMESH KUMAR GUPTA

The creative artist of our age has to become a god, independent of his creation, revealing his omnipresence through a pervasive insinuation of his compassion or understanding of all his characters, through the varying tensions of their lives in search of personal relations. [1]

The most distinguished humanist of today is Dr Mulk Raj Anand, an internationally reputed Indo-Anglian novelist, short-story writer, essayist, art critic and poet. Mr Anand s emphasis on the dignity of man irrespective of caste, creed and wealth, his plea for the exercise of compassion as a living value, his conception of the whole man, the deep significance he attaches to art and poetry as instruments for developing whole men, his crusade against superstition, feudalism, and imperialism these are some of the chief characteristics of his humanism. The theme and subjects of Anand are chiefly aimed at portraying the contemporary social situation as seen and felt by the individual. More often than not, Anand s individual finds himself in an unenviable circumstance, being a prey of feeble traditions and savage customs, a defiled social order or a cruel administration. Delineating graphically the helpless individual in his pitiful and helpless state, Anand aims at touching the humanist chords of the reader s heart, with a message perhaps that only a concerted effort can examine the non-too-gay present social situation. Mr S. Lakshman Shastry, the editor of the *Contemporary Indian Literature*, rightly observes:

> Dr Mulk Raj Anand is a unique type of optimistic humanist who is capable to move the most pessimistic man to action. He is a very sensitive lover of all that is good and lovable on earth good books, fine pieces of art, good manners. He stands for lasting peace and friendly relations between nations. At the same time he is also ruthless critic of all that is worn-out and decaying-dehumanising and degrading customs, manners, outdated social and political institutions, reactionary thoughts and ideologies. As a disciple of Tagore and Nehru, Dr Anand has made painstaking efforts to understand the soul of this land which has been expressing itself through Indian thought and Indian culture. It appears to us that it is the profound knowledge of Indian mind on the one hand, and critical assessment of the various outdated social systems and institutions on the other, that has made Anand an uncompromising agitator and organiser.[2]

Anand is thus a humanist to the core. It is his constant faith in humanism that has perhaps made him a lovable man with infinite charm and several interests. He is a true friend, a tireless worker, an excited organiser, a prolific writer, an unceasing champion of the cause of the poor and the submissive, a savage combatant against inequality and injustice, and above all, a trustworthy humanist with endless faith in man and creative arts on which his expectations are made evident by his letter of 3rd Oct., 1968 to G.S. Balrama Gupta:

> [...] if the 21st century is to be born, we must understand each other s humanness and cultivate the arts through which we may achieve the universal basis for no war, against stupidity, malice, aforethought and meanness of mind.

Anand exposes the contemporary situation through an analysis of the predicament of the men and women he knows. Anand saw India in terms of enslavement, caste, poverty, religious archaism, saluted the enduring heroism of the poor and oppression of the women. The women that reside in Anand s world are all preys of habit where man is ascribed the pride of place and thus allowed the socio-cultural confirmation of the female banishment. *The Old Woman and the Cow* presents the story of Gauri, a meek and gentle country-woman who suffers silently all the hardships and injustices imposed on her by her mother, mother-in-law, and even her husband till she meets the enlightened city doctor, colonel Mahindra, under whose influence she grows glowingly conscious of her intrinsic worth as an independent individual. The leitmotif of this novel develops in Gauri s journey to emancipation. She is married to Panchi, the holy bull. Gauri, the gentle Cow wanders from Piplan Kalan to Chota Piplan, symbolises a considerable fall in her destiny. Gauri s husband Panchi, also tries to free himself from the crushing and debasing influence of his uncle and aunt and the entire village bent on fault-finding and agitating him, but he fails. But his very combat, just as Gauri s, attracts our sympathy.

Anand s humanistic note in *The Old Woman and the Cow* is obvious that presents the strong plea for the identification and approval of women s rights. The novelist s sense of disbelief in the Christian perspective of vice, his emphasis on the value of compassion in human affinities, his criticism of the cash-bond, and his usual reproof of uncritical faith in superstition, Karma, and God these are the humanistic notes that form the plot of this novel.

In our conventional socio-cultural milieu the woman remains unrealized, trapped, caged and oppressed. That women need equality with men is the chief principle of Anand s humanism which constructs the plot of this novel. The novelist presents the treatments of man s ideas and actions in respect of woman. Gauri s whole life is a tale of torture and trauma. The crowded and obstructed atmosphere of the joint family does not allot a room for making love between Gauri and her husband. She does nothing but groans and moans under the distress of male chauvinism. She is abidingly blamed of being an inauspicious creature, liable not only for the mishaps of the family but also for the drought in the village. Kesari, the traditional mother-in-law, does not want to loosen her hold on Panchi and continues to despise and distress Gauri. She is helpless. She finds a little love and tenderness in the corner of her husband s heart. Her husband, Panchi, is also a prey of the stratagems of the envious Kesari and artful Mola Ram. Despite his occasional love and compassion for Gauri, he is mostly seen savage peasant, a wild bull whose gruesome tendency comes in constant clash with Gauri s gentle nature. It is obvious in these lines:

> [...] there was the prospect of the prize of a girl a girl whom he could fold in his arms at night and kick during the day [...]. (*The Old Woman and the Cow*, 5)

Panchi is a weak husband. He does not consider the veritable predicament of his wife, Gauri. He becomes a victim of Kesari s machination. Kesari makes him believe that Gauri is *de facto* inauspicious and immoral. But it is Gauri who is probably succeeded in mollifying Panchi through her mere affection and endurance. Consequently she is conceived and becomes teemful. But it does not last for long. Gauri is bartered away by a malice and licentious uncle, Amru and a greedy mother, Lakshmi, for money and wiping out of mortgage on two houses and a cow, to the old and rude widower Seth Jai Ram Das in Hoshiarpur. She gets free from the Seth s house to Dr Mahindra s Hospital, with fever and malady and now she feels free from the clutches of the old Seth who entices her to live as his wife. Here she contends with Dr Batra, a beastly debauchee. Dr Mahindra s gentle behaviour and reformist ideas bring about a transformation in her. Her life takes a constant change in the company of Dr Mahindra. Now she has been changed from gentle cow to a self-willed woman with her own individuality. Once getting a chance she goes back to her husband but Panchi mistrusts her virginity in that she passed some days with the Seth Jai Ram Das and Dr Mahindra. Hence, he scolds and strikes her and gives order to desert his house. But Gauri is no longer a passive creature to avow this kind of behaviour. So she reacts and says:

> If I am a curse on you, I will go away [...]. And if you strike me again, I will hit you back. (*Ibid.*, 282-83)

Here Anand presents the symbolic aspect of modern women who are conscious of their rights and individualities. What she was now she is not. She is no longer a gentle cow. She takes compact decisions and raises the reasonable facts:

> He (Panchi) is not foolish. He is a weak, spoilt creature [...]. He pretended to be a lion among the men of the

> village: But really he is a coward: They are telling him that Ram turned out Sita because everyone doubted her chastity during her stay with Ravana: [...] I am not Sita that the earth will open up and swallow me. I shall just go and be forgotten of him [...]. (*Ibid.*, 283)

Gauri gets away from her husband s life and starts a new life of dedication to the dejected, poor and wretched.

Another aspect of Anand s humanistic note in this novel is the emphasis on the demand for deserting pain and barbarity and exercising mollification and softness. The novelist does this by depicting a true scene of the gloomy plot against which the tragedy of the novel takes place. At whatever place Gauri goes she meets with savage suffering but it is only Dr Mahindra who gives her solace. She tries to go to her every kith and kin for her shelter but she is hurt by each of them. They take rest after doing away with her from their house. Even her husband does it whom Gauri truly loves. Panchi thinks that she is his wife and he is her lord so he can hit and kick her. Kesari, aunt-in-law, tortures her upto the very end by using the envious conduct and by instigating Panchi against her. Lakshmi and Amru love their property more than their daughter so they sell her away to a sixty-year old Seth. Gauri does face all the severe tests in her life but thanks to Dr Mahindra who is sympathetic to her. As usual in India, rains fail and drought takes its place and it raises in the psychics of the villagers that unpropitious happening is due to Gauri. And thus the mishap instigates the villagers to their savagery. Even Gauri thinks that her husband, Panchi, would have probably sent her away due to his miseries and mishaps. Mr Anand explicates it through a minor character of the novel Rafique Chacha and indicates that poverty need not make people savage. Rafique Chacha is a poor man, but he is by nature gentle and keeps his goodness in spite of all miseries. He is kind enough to ask Panchi and his wife, Gauri, to come and live with him. He does not leave any attempt to make their lives lively and delightful. But Dr Mahindra s solace and generosity make Gauri a hopeful woman. Due to Lakshmi s and Amru s greed for money Gauri faces with hardships. Dr Mahindra tries to up with the veritable evil of money and tells Lakshmi how people s greed for money, power, possession and property has dominated in their lives:

> [...] we pile up gold upon gold; silver upon silver [...] the Sethias, who buy and sell, have brought falsity into the life of the village. In the old days, there was often scarcity. But as no one owned the land, the five elders could give fertile land to whoever complained that his land was fallow [...]. And there was milk and butter and whey [...]. Now, every peasant owns his land and can sell it [...]. And cash has become more valuable than the earth. And thus there is wretchedness everywhere. Your Amru turns crook and you sell your daughter, even as folks in Gorakhpur district of Uttar Pradesh are selling their daughters. (*Ibid.*, 239-40)

Lakshmi s lure for money, the new god induces her to sell away her daughter. Even the hillmen do not flee from the enticement of money, and its consequences are calamitous. Lakshmi says to the city confectioner:

> [...] Womcn always taught men to love [...]. But when you shopkeepers came with your money you taught us hill people to buy and sell girls [...]. I am not ashamed of having gone to bed with men, but I am ashamed that I had to sell my daughter [...]. (*Ibid.*, 226)

The novelist tries to combat against the man s faith in charms and omens, his power, possession, money, Karma, and God all age-old notions which impedes the development of the people. The denizens of the village are the victims of superstitions. Panchi sometimes feels it nugatory to believe in superstitions but he is not completely got rid of it only because he considers the destiny of Gauri who is a prey of mishaps. Kesari thinks that these mishaps are due to the wrong stars of Gauri. Compelled by the circumstances Gauri herself thinks that she is probably an inauspicious woman as blamed by all. Like her husband, Gauri also believes in destiny and God, since she artlessly thinks that a day will come when she will be free from the reward of sufferings imposed by the kith and kin and the villagers. She contemplates that there is no means or no way for proving her virginity, for the Mother Earth would not open up and swallow her hence she decides to work out her own dirting herself. Here the novelist indicates that man must rely on himself for his liveliness rather than on luck or God. Anand does not believe in the dogma of rebirth which is the mythical aspect of our Indian 'religio-reliance.' That is why the novelist interprets it through Dr Mahindra:

> [...] the idea of deserving a higher birth, as a reward for good or bad deeds is, to my thinking, a myth promoted to keep men and women at work for the slave-drivers [...]. It is true that at the back of all wretchedness, there is the soul of man. And the soul remains when the wretchedness has passed [...] so the deepest good builds on the deepest human being, the whole man [...]. Any how, there is no question of rebirth. (*Ibid.*, 243)

Initially we find in the novel that Mr Anand presents a realistic picture of Gauri's sufferings. Gauri, a good and gentle woman, is aptly compared to a cow, for her endurance and immolation. The novelist again tries to evince the changes that come about in her. The credit goes to Dr Mahindra who has influenced her life therefore she realises that her salvation does not remain in her endurance and obedience to an age-old corrupted society, but in an active opposition to it. Her company with Dr Mahindra opens out a new horizon of life. Gauri, on this very ground, defies her family, wrenches herself from it completely and starts to live a new life on a new ground. The whole plot is based on realism. The characters do not present only realistic ideas but they also depict the humanistic note of the novelist. Panchi, Lakshmi, Amru, Kesari, Mola Ram, Dr Batra all are meant to indicate the age-old victims of Indian family and society—savage, impassive and superstitious. Dr Mahindra tries to implant humanist ideas in Gauri by which she evinces how a person needs to depend on himself rather than on God for constructing his fate. The novelist tries to combat against falsity and hypocrisy, savagery and insensibility, and a defense of love and compassion, and all that goes to make man's life gaysome and lenient.

In this novel we find the whole process of the change of woman from a puppet in man's hands to the state of an independent woman who asserts her equal rights with man and demands recognition as such. The novelist adroitly makes use of the old myth of the *Ramayana* and suggests how it is no longer possible for man either to keep woman suppressed or to neglect her lawful liberty, equality, identity and individuality. The emphasis for the amelioration of woman is one of the significant aspects of Anand s humanism. Dr P.T. Raju, a reputed thinker, rightly says that the present age is an age of humanism. [3] In the works of Dr Anand are avowedly inspired by his compassion:

> And as my media as a writer were the memory and imagination, the substance of my work became the whole man, and the whole gamut of human relationships, rather than only one single part of it.[4]

We see that man is the chief exponent of humanism. The novelist says that it means what humanism has meant all along generally illumination or enlightenment in the interest of man, true to his highest nature and his noblest vision. [5] This way, man is the measure of all things. [6]

NOTES AND REFERENCES

1. Mulk Raj Anand, Old Myths and New Myths: Recital *Versus* Novel, *Indian Literature of the Past Fifty Years* (ed. C.D. Narasimhaiah, Mysore, 1970), 119.
2. S. Lakshman Shastry, A Few Words About This Issue (Editorial), *Contemporary Indian Literature*, November-December, 1965, 10.
3. P.T. Raju, *The Concept of Man*, ed. S. Radhakrishnan and P.T. Raju (London, 1960), 15.
4. M.R. Anand, Apology for Heroism (Bombay, 1957), 18.
5. M.R. Anand, *Lines Written to an Indian Air* (Bombay, 1949), 7.
6. N.T. Stace, *A Critical History of Greek Philosophy* (London, 1962), 123.

7

Humour and Irony in the Pre-Independence Novels of Mulk Raj Anand

ASHOK KUMAR BACHCHAN

The comic element in literature aims at amusing or exciting mirth in the reader or audience and both wit and humour are species of the comic. While wit consists in verbal ingenuity or inventiveness of an intelligent mind and usually evokes a laugh or smile without malice, humour has its genesis in comical eccentricity and may be ascribed to a comic speech, appearance or mode of behaviour. Wit is always verbal whereas humour has a much broader range of reference. Humour evokes sympathetic laughter.

Humour is related to amusement or laughter. It may be defined as the capacity to cause or feel amusement. [1] However, humour has different connotations on different occasions. In the Medieval or Jonsonian sense it stands for a particular idiosyncrasy or mentality peculiar to a particular person, the dominance of one particular passion, the drive of one particular disposition in a person. [2] What we mean by humour in the present context is the creation or evocation, by means of words, gestures or actions, of a pleasing or happy sensation which necessarily leads to the relaxation of tension. There is something spontaneous about humour, it does not lose its natural or affectionate quality.

Irony, on the other hand, is an intellectual phenomenon. It requires a certain degree of intelligence, of mental effort, of intellectual exercise to be able to produce irony. Irony, is a rhetorical device that implies two levels of the meaning of a statement, the first level of the meaning appearing to be simple and direct while the other going by implication or suggestion. Irony consists in an act of dissembling or dissimulation. While people speak of verbal irony, dramatic irony or the irony of fate or situation, the denomination that is common to all these varieties is the sharpness of contrast between what is stated and what is implied, between seeming and being.

Dr Anand s irony is definitely not so severe as that of Jonathan Swift or Alexander Pope; it is gentle and piercing. His sympathy is reserved for the poor and the downtrodden and, more often than not, he directs the shafts of his irony towards the well-to-do upper class Indian people and the oppressive English folk that are supercilious and contemptuous. Sometimes he exposes even the poor people who believe in the working of fate. At the same time, he laughs at the absurdities, incongruities and eccentricities in an individual or a society or a political system. It is really remarkable that besides being a humanist and realist, he manages to be a humorist. Without his sense of humour Anand might have been a mere propagandist, as some of his critics try to label him.

Untouchable is certainly a dirge on the predicament of the outcastes in India but there is still an unmistakable streak of irony and humour in this novel. We laugh at the gibes and strictures of Gulabo, a termagant washerwoman, at the hypocrisy of Pundit Kalinath who attempts to seduce Bakha s sister, Sohini. The incessant shower of swear-words, abuses and eccentric utterances of some characters also create humour on certain occasions in the novel.

The irony lies in the fact that small children of the upper caste are more reasonable than grown-up people in their society. The former do not mind if Bakha touches them while playing hockey, but the latter raise a hullabaloo if Bakha happens to touch them by chance. Small children appear to be more considerate than their elders. Anand does not spare even the outcastes who are habituated to live in slush and filth. Lakha, Rakha and many like them have dirty habits. Anand s humour is not Chaucerian because at times he severely attacks the rotten conventionalism as well as the loss of human values in the modern westerners or their followers in the East.

Mulk Raj Anand is basically an iconoclast. He is against orthodoxy and bigotry in any religion whether it be Hindu, Muslim, Sikh, or Christian. Bakha is led astray by colonel Hutchinson who wants to convert him into Christian. Anand treats this episode very ironically and is of the opinion that one does not become religious simply by performing a lot of religious rites day in and day out, caring not a whit for the suffering humanity. Colonel Hutchinson, who wants to fulfil his mission by converting a low-caste Hindu boy to Christianity is as despicable as the hypocrite lecher, Pundit Kalinath. The hollow religious notion of a Hindu housewife has been railed at in the episode in which Bakha is despised as a dog although he cleans her street while she holds a deceptive Sadhu in high esteem.

The statement of the poet, in *Untouchable,* who wants to explain the drawbacks of Hinduism is deeply sarcastic. The monist concept of Shankaracharya has been railed upon in the following passage:

> There has been only one man in India who believed this world to be illusory Shankaracharya. But he was consumptive and that made him neurotic. Early European scholars could not get hold of the original texts of the Upanishads. So they kept on interpreting Indian thought from the commentaries of Shankaracharya. It was as if in order to give a philosophical background to their exploitation of India that they ingeniously concocted a nice little fairy-story: You don t believe in this world: to you all this is Maya. Let us look after your country for you and you can dedicate yourself to achieving nirvana. [3]

A person considering religion as a means for earning gold, like the pardoner in Chaucer s *Canterbury Tales,* deceives people talking about death, rebirth, illusion, salvation, righteousness and sin without actually knowing about them. Such men have been severely dealt with in such passages. What Jung means by collective Unconscious , Shankaracharya means by his Akeshwarvad. Had we caught the true spirit of this belief, there would emerge no classes, castes and creeds to divide and separate man from man. It is also very humorous that colonel Hutchinson who sets out to propagate Christianity cows down before his vociferous wife. Thus *Untouchable* has some good examples of humour and irony.

Munoo, the chief protagonist in *Coolie,* like the heroes of picaresque novels *i.e.,* Fielding s *Tom Jones,* Dickens s *David Copperfield* and Mark Twain s *Tom Sawyer* and *Huckleberry Finn,* exposes the feudal tyranny, inequitable social distribution, incongruities and inconsistencies prevailing all-around him. It is an irony of fate that in search of relief, love and livelihood, he moves from place to place, but the changed situation proves to be worse for him.

Munoo escapes his nagging aunt only to fall in the grip of a still worse woman, Bibi Uttam Kaur. Mrs Maimwaring is fascinated by the physical grace of the boy but fails to know his agonies and strifes, his damaged lungs and his sinister consumption. There are certain highly dramatic situations in the novel; Mr England s visit to the Bank Babu s house is one of them. The superimposed gravity of Mr England and the affected humility of the Bank Babu create humour.

It is deeply ironical that wherever Munoo goes, he brings ill luck. Babu Nathu Ram fails to win Mr England s favour and Prabha is deceived by his partner, Ganpat and goes bankrupt. A Hindu-Muslim riot begins during a strike in the cotton mill in Bombay where Munoo lives with Hari and his wife, Lakshmi. He is hit by the car of Mrs Maimwaring who takes him to Simla. After he comes round, he has to pull rickshaw for the sake of Mrs Maimwaring and this aggravates his consumption, and ultimately, he succumbs to it. At one stage Munoo ponders over his ill luck:

> Am I really ominous? he asked himself, My father died when I was born, and then my mother, and I brought misfortune to Hari now. If I am ominous why don t I die? [4]

But Munoo does not suffer due to chance or fate as the characters of Hardy do; rather his suffering ensures from the inequality both social and economic. He suffers at the hands of Indian masters and even his fellow workers more than he does at the hands of his English masters. In *Coolie,* Anand attacks the rich who exploit their fellow Indians and are not at ease with people of their own class:

> The rich don t really want to mix with each other. The women perspire in their furs and their underclothes get wet. And the men are uncomfortable in their tight trousers as they flirt with other men s wives. Then they say how smart it all was as they drink tea at Davico s while you starve. (312)

Anand considers a change of heart necessary for recalling human values. The rich, he thinks, are too dazzled by luxuries to be aware of the suffering of those who die from hunger and deprivation. They seem to have lost all moral and human values and they follow the materialistic ways of the westerners to whom carnal pleasures contain the seed of all happiness. They do not understand the meaning of ideal human relationship based on selfless love. Mrs Maimwaring s concept of Indian life, that it is so full of luxuries and so cheap, has essentially a tinge of irony:

> India was one of the places in the world where one could come into dress and leave the discarded garments in a heap on the floor, to be collected and folded away by the servants [...]. Why here were all the luxuries and amenities of the west at the knock down prices of the East, so that even Golders, Green and Ealing lived like Mayfair and Picadilly. (301-02)

Some repeated abuses and swear words produce humour in *Coolie.* The characters like Sir Todar Mal, his wife and his Inspector son are severely treated in the novel. They like to flatter the English rulers and are more supercilious to their fellow countrymen than any white man could be. They are the immediate butts of irony and stocks of humour. On the whole there is little scope of humour in *Coolie* in which the hero is driven to endless sufferings until he dies.

Two Leaves and a Bud is notable for its tragic irony. Gangu leaves his village with a rainbow dream of prosperity, but at the mere touch of the crude realities of life at Macpherson Tea Estate in Assam, his dream is shattered into bits. His life is stormed by disasters. First of all his wife dies of diarrhoea and at last he is shot dead by Reggie Hunt who wanted to seduce his young daughter. The immediate object of Anand s irony and sarcasm are the white-skinned people who are diabolical at heart. With an exception of De La Harve, they all are shorn of human qualities. Even the unsympathetic natives like Buta Sardar and Shashi Bhushan shrink away from the bare minimum human responsibility when calamity befalls Gangu.

The first thing Gangu s wife, Sajni, does after reaching Assam is to pray to Lord Shiva of Nandi Parbat to keep her family safe and happy but, ironically enough, her family gets destroyed. Gangu considers Leila a gift of Sajni but she gives him the gift of death at the end.

There is an ironical contrast between the luxurious life of the English people and the hard life of the coolies at the Macpherson Tea Estate. Anand, sometimes, mocks at the hollow pomp and show of the white people. In the following passage, Sir Geoffrey Boyd, the Governor of Assam Tea Estate, is described in an ironical vein:

> It was the theory of late Lord Curzon, His Excellency had written to Croft-Cooke, that the orientals had a tremendous regard for pomp and show. And they like their kings to be Great and Marvellous, and their Queens to be truly spectacular and Beautiful!
>
> His Excellency had forgotten that he was hardly five foot five, that he had become grey-haired through long service in the I.C.S. and according to his friends, looked more like an insurance agent, in spite of his high collar and pince-nez, than like the Maharajah of Patiala or Akbar the Great Mogul, and that his wife, Her Excellency, Lady Lucy Boyd, had shrivelled up through her long stay in the heart of India and was certainly, not in any way like the Queen of Sheba or Noormahal.[5]

To Anand, a good writer is essentially magnanimous, enjoying a high pedestal, and is precisely the man who can encompass the whole of life. [6] As the novels of the first phase deal with serious socio-economic problems, there is limited scope for humour and irony in them. Anand s central concern is the immediate as well as ultimate sorrows confronted by human beings rather than their petty aspirations and their negligible sources of happiness. *Two Leaves and a Bud* ends on a pathetic note of irony when the Devil incarnate Reggie Hunt is released by the English Judges while he is the actual murderer of Gangu.

The Big Heart deals with the theme of the clash between tradition and modernity. It presents a chaotic society which is confused about the benefits and disadvantages of heavy machines. The novelist and his spokesmen, Ananta and Puran Singh Bhagat, see the evils of the machine age, writes Saros Cowasjee, and the benefits of the old way of life; they realise that the older order is obsolete in a country on the verge of a vast social, economic and political change. [7]

There are a few characters and situations that arouse laughter and point at some absurdities of human nature in *The Big Heart.* Murlidhar, the lecherous and materialistic landlord, is pooh-poohed for neglecting his poor relatives for introducing new heavy machines and for having illicit relationship with his daughter-in-law. The incident of beggars struggling and sweating for puris fallen on a stinking rubbish-heap very ironically reveals the tyranny of the British rule and capitalism.

Ananta s pet slogan, There is no talk of money one must have a big heart; Ralia s comment on electricity and Rail Injan and Janki s mockery of Ananta s business, are some good examples of light humour in an otherwise grim novel. Uncle Viroo s belief sow good deeds and you will reap good deeds gets ironically defeated in the case of Ananta who, despite his altruistic ideals and deeds, is murdered ruthlessly by his bosom friend Ralia.

Janki s pathetic account of herself in the following passage, in fact, hints at the exploitation of women in the conservative Indian society:

> I have certainly begun to think clearly of all those who deny us freedom. First of all my parents who created me not because they loved each other but because they considered it their duty, and who regarded me, when I was born, as a curse because I was a girl. Then my husband and his relations, who were more

> concerned with dowry I brought than with me. Later, when the owner of my house had died, society considered me as one who should be dead to all impulses and live only to worship the memory of my dead lord and master. Do you (Ananta) remember the things that were said all over Punjab because I ran away with you? The followers of the Mahatma in Bombai who believed in freedom, yet despised me because I was not married to you.[8]

Anand makes a plea for widow-remarriage which is considered an unpardonable sin in the caste Hindu society. He has Swiftian hatred for all kinds of hypocrisy either in an individual or in a social or religious system. In Author s note in *The Big Heart,* he writes:

> *The Big Heart* was written, from the torment of living between two worlds one not quite dead and the other refusing to be born! And it is precious to me for the shelter it gave me as a half-way house before facing other storms. (31)

In fact, *The Big Heart,* despite its lack of mirth and jubilation, is full of ironical shafts against everything wrong in individuals, society, religion, tradition and politics.

Lal Singh, the hero of *The Village,* is diametrically opposite in nature to Munoo, Gangu or Bakha. He has resolved to fight against hypocrisy in society, culture, politics and the moral tradition of India during 1920s. He ridicules Mahant Nandgir, the twin brother of libidinous Pundit Kalinath in *Untouchable,* he is at once a great lecher, a glutton and a bibulous drunkard, who is, ironically enough, the law-giver of the village in both social and religious matters. He and many of his type *i.e.,* the landlord, the moneylender, the trader, the lawyer and the British ruler, exploit the poor, ignorant, innocent but superstitious village folk.

Lal Singh grows bitterly critical about the elders of the society who:

> [...] were always forbidding you to do this and that, these elders, always curtailing your liberty. Always frustrating your desires. You could not even laugh in their presence. You had to join your hands gravely

> and say, I fall at your feet. And they were ridiculous fools, ugly uncouth lumps of flesh, wide-eyed, open-mouthed simpletons, saying prayers and mentioning the name of god all day, even as they lasciviously eyed the young girls passing in the bazaar.[9]

It is actually a humorous caricature of the village elders who preach to others what they themselves never pay heed to. Lal Singh makes a mockery of the hollowness of Sikh religion when he eats meat from a Muslim cook-shop, cuts his long hair which he considers a forest of tangled overgrowth and because of the outward form of Sikh religion calls it a religion of Donkeys; a religion of bullocks as people with blind faith never try to reason out the impracticality of Katch, Kara, Kirpan, Kesh and Kanga in the modern times. To him, these things are anachronistic and are only the signs of religious fanaticism.

There are numerous ludicrous characters and situations in the novel which draw out humour and irony. Dr Anand attacks the incongruous and anachronistic elements of old conventions and tradition. The miserly landlord, Sardar Harbans Singh, and the artful moneylender, Chaman Lal, are thoroughly exposed. The author s objectivity lies, however, in his attempt to uphold many good elements of tradition which lay stress on integrity, tenacity, courage and faith. The sense of unity and the joy de vivre of village-life are artistically presented.

Across the Black Waters, the second of the Lal Singh trilogy, *The Village* being the first, is a major war-novel among Indian-English novels. In it Lal Singh s escape from his village symbolises an escape from the suicidal grips of rused traditional beliefs and customs. The whole plot revolves round Lal Singh s regiment disembarking at Marseilles to fight in Flanders, and lastly, his imprisonment in Germany.

During his stay in Britain and France, Lal Singh is highly impressed by the cleanliness and brotherhood of the Europeans and praises the freedom of women there and is shocked by their exploitation in India. The following accounts of Lal Singh are tinged with humour and irony:

> Lalu could not keep his eyes off the smiling, pretty-frocked girls with breasts half showing, bright and gleaming with [...] happiness [...] such a contrast to the

> sedate Indian women who seemed to grow old before they were young, fabby and tired [...] why even the matrons here were dressed up and not content to remain unadorned like Indian wives, who thought that there was a greater dignity in neglecting themselves after they had had a child or two.[10]

Back at home, Lalu remembers, you must always put on a miserable expression and remain miserable, quiet in the presence of your elders that is respect. And of course, you must never commit the crime of being happy. [11]

In Europe, Lal Singh is disillusioned and his prejudice against European people is dispelled after he comes across the kind and noble Capt. Owen and French farmer s anguished wife. Lance-corporal Lok Nath (with his language larded with abuses) and Subhash Singh (with his toughness towards Lalu) are characters lying in ironical contrast. Anand brings out the crookedness and absurdities of human nature with the help of irony.

Although Anand had a brief sojourn in the University trenches during his visit to Spain to join the International Brigade while the Spanish Civil War was going on, he had many first hand descriptions of war in his mind which as a boy he had heard in his father s regiment. This is what makes his novel as effective and artistic as Crane s *The Red Badge of Courage* and E.M. Remarque s *All Quiet on the Western Front.*

There are some interludes of light humour in *Across the Black Waters.* It is a tragic irony that Lachman Singh receives posthumously the award of the Indian order of Merit. The following duet improvised by Lalu and his friends about a sepoy and his sweetheart Harnami is comic in vein.

> I want a pair of shoes
> [...] vary Harnam Singh
> Oh, I shall fetch for you
> A pair of fine shoes, with
> high heels, Ni Harnamie. (235)

Ironically enough, the lady is completely oblivious of the fact of death which her lover must face in the battle-field. The description of traitors in Hindustani Army working in favour of the Germans is very sarcastic.

We come across numerous instances of irony and humour in *The Sword and the Sickle.* The double-facedness of Count or Kunwar Ramphal Singh and the Malvolian seriousness of Prof. Verma remind the reader of Chaucer s Tales and of Shakespeare s comedies. Ramphal Singh is called a quick-witted buffoon ; comrade Ram Din looks like a camel, Pandit Ram Kumar Mishra is a victim of his wife s broom for going to bed with a cobbler woman and comrade Gupta has a fair monkeyish face with rare blue eye which are brimming over with mischief attempt to show communism in a ludicrous light and to point out the limitations of Gandhism is entertaining and somewhat farcical.

The European life-style in the household of Pandit Moti Lal Nehru and preaching as well as practice of simplicity by Gandhiji and his followers, the watering of flowers and plying primitive spinning wheels present humorous and ironical contrasts. M.K. Naik poses a series of questions[12] about the confused handling of the theme of anti-feudalism by Anand.

Lal Singh, an experienced and mature man that he is, wavers because he knows well that to make an enduring sheet the thread should be twisted at both ends. So his confusion is the sure sign of his growing worldly wisdom. Lal Singh is actually fed up with political isms and their limitations and so chooses to live peacefully with his beloved wife, Maya.

In fact, humour and irony are not the chief attributes of Mulk Raj Anand s language but he does use them wherever necessary. His use of irony and humour depends on the demand of his theme, plot, structure and, above all, the effective and artistic presentation of Indian life in his novels.

REFERENCES

1. A.S. Hornby (Ed.), *Oxford Advanced Learner s Dictionary of Current English* (London, 1974), 424.
2. Herbert Read, *English Prose Style* (Ludhiana, 1968), 162.
3. M.R. Anand, *Untouchable* (Arnold Heinemann, 1984), 170.
4. M.R. Anand, *Coolie* (Bombay, 1971), 217.
5. M.R. Anand, *Two Leaves and a Bud* (Arnold Heinemann, 1983), 251-52.
6. M.R. Anand, *Apology for Heroism* (Bombay, 1946), 9.
7. Saros Cowasjee, An Introduction to *The Big Heart* (Arnold Heinemann, 1980), 1.

8. M.R. Anand, *The Big Heart* (Arnold Heinemann, 1980), 174.
9. M.R. Anand, *The Village* (Bombay, 1939), 55.
10. M.R. Anand, *Across the Black Waters* (Bombay, 1941), 14.
11. *Ibid.*, 41.
12. M.K. Naik, *Mulk Raj Anand* (Arnold Heinemann, 1973), 74-75.

8

Individual versus Society in the Novels of Mulk Raj Anand and Anita Desai

BINOD MISHRA

Literature and society complement each other the way human heart and mind do. The superiority of one upon the other cannot be established in a hurry. Literature records dreams and desires, fears and furies, fact and fiction in its minutest details to soothe and soften mankind in hours of agony and anguish. It also creates the background of numberless games, which decide the fate of individuals and of society. It brings a change, which keeps germinating, in the minds of man for years. The saga of man s emergence from the savage to the civilized stage is nothing but the result of the transforming power of literature.

Mulk Raj Anand and Anita Desai, the two prolific practitioners of Indian writing in English, through their novels, have described the transformation of Indian life and society in a very subtle manner. Their portrayal of a variety of characters shows not only the hue and cry of individual against system but also the whispering notes which the individuals feel but fail to hum against the noises of the maddening crowd.

The paper endeavours to trace the impact of the restrictions imposed by society on individuals as delineated in the works of two novelists. The reaction of their characters to the social issues bespeaks the exciting and the inspiring tale of their struggle and quest. The growing concern of Anand and Anita for their characters in this hydra-headed world does not go a waste but keeps mankind reminding of its hush-hush hissings.

Both Anand and Anita Desai through their novels show how their characters in their search for identity find themselves at war with society, the masses. Their desire to earmark a little space in this vast world mars their hopes and harmony offering them pains and perils in return. In their struggle they shine forth like gold in furnace.

Cry, the Peacock (1963), the first novel by Anita Desai, depicts an individual s cries against the mass in general and Maya-Gautam s incoherent marital life in particular. Their marriage grounded upon the friendship of Maya s father and Gautama fails to obtain the test of each other s trust and they become poles apart. The artist in Maya covets for the sensations of life, which cannot be lived on her own terms. Gautama s legal quibbles fail to find any room in Maya s heart. The impediments in their relationship are born of the lack of understanding each other s waves. Maya s parental passion and Gautama s garrulous grudges seem never to end and only widen the cleavage between them. Gautama tries to console and convince Maya but fails to fulfil even her carnal desires. As a result, Maya feels herself an appendage not only on her husband but also on his family. To attach at least some sense of significance to her injured self, Maya builds a world of flora and fauna. She alienates herself not only from Gautama and his family members but also from Leila and Pom, her one-time friends. She turns inward and nauseates to find the depletion even there. Unlike Rosie in R.K. Narayan s *The Guide*, Maya does not believe in falling into the arms of someone who soothes her physically and mentally. Rather Maya s agonized self can get peace only by killing her husband in a vindictive rage. Maya, the peacock finally fulminates her furious cries and vindicates herself. The novel, though a love-hate tragedy at large, appears as an individual s outburst against society:

> Now that I understand their call, I wept for them, and wept for myself, knowing their words to be mine.[1]

In *Voices in the City* (1965), Anita discusses the plight of a sensitive intellectual woman who fights against the hostile family only to triumph after her death. The voices of Monisha, the heroine of the novel are subdued by the authoritative society represented by her in-laws. Neither the husband nor the members of his family sympathize with Monisha and she ends her alienation by burning herself to death. The other characters namely Nirode and Amla are also snubbed. Monisha s brother, Nirode, is an artist who meets failure one after another. Not only Monisha but also Nirode, Amla and Maya dwindle into insignificance in their fight against society. Nirode works in a newspaper office and shuns his job because of his dissatisfaction. He edits a literary magazine named Voice which fails to lend the ears of the city-dwellers and still he writes a play only to taste another sting of failure. Nirode s creative waves have very few takers. He fails and fritters. At one place, he admits:

> I want to move from failure to failure, step by step, to rock bottom. I want to explore that depth.[2]

Nirode is soon disillusioned with life as Monisha s death ultimately seals his medium for communication. His younger sister Amla, trained as a commercial artist in Bombay comes to Calcutta to join an advertisement firm. Notionally different from Monisha and Nirode she attends parties and dances to the tune of time but realizes lately that happiness was but an occasional episode in the general drama of pain. She, too, grouches in anguish:

> this city, this city of yours, it conspires against all who wish to enjoy it [...].[3]

Through the characters of Nirode, Monisha, Amla and Maya, Anita hints at individual consciousness but it also depicts the consciousness of a world that is both real and unreal. The city of Calcutta represents a big world, a greater society where the individual s voices are always choked only to be yoked with violence in the form of goddess Kali, which the city symbolizes.

Where Shall We Go This Summer (1982) depicts an individual s fight against society more poignantly. The novel deals with the agony of the middle-aged heroine, Sita who wants to live life at her own costs. Sita has high expectations of life and her expectations receive a jolt as she fails to adjust herself with her husband and his family. Her marriage with Raman was not a marriage of true minds. Raman, a businessman failed to feel the weariness, the fever and the fret, which Sita experiences behind the curtains of his house. Her desire to live live independently forces Raman to live with her separately in another flat. But here again she lives unhappily. Having given birth to four issues, now she shows signs of boredom when she becomes pregnant for the fifth time. She smokes all through the night and shows her reluctance to deliver the fifth child. Her abnormal behaviour surprises every one. She decides to go to Manori, an island where she had spent her childhood under the shadow of her father. Her father, a public figure, had spent his entire life on the island calling it Jeevan Ashram.

The island also does not extenuate her whimsical approach and she appears mad to Moses and his friends. Her children also stand up against her and want to return to their father in Bombay. When Raman reaches the island, Sita receives a blow and is full of shame and frustration. She has come to realize that life cannot be lived on one s own terms and decides to go with Raman who is a symbol of security to her. She reconciles in the end, no doubt, but the way she expresses her crisis of life not lived, give a hint at her individuation:

> I thought I could live with you and travel alone mentally, emotionally. But after that day, that wasn t enough. I had to stay whole, I had to.[4]

Sita s return to Raman may at surface level appear to be her defeat but at the deeper level, there is a delight in this defeat. Defeat or win in private life has no substance. Her return to Bombay is a possible push towards rejuvenation. Her life on the island is an exile, which has uprooted her from her setting. And this is why Usha Bande, a noted critic justifies Sita s compromise in the following way:

> Acceptance shows growth ripeness; it implies the process of actualization. The ability to connect the fragments of life and achieve an integration, will perhaps enable her to realize her place and experience herself as a part of a larger whole.[5]

Anita shows the fight between the individuals and society more clearly in one of her later novels, *In Custody* (1984), which has been considered more individual, less generalized and conventional than her earliest fiction. [6] The hero of the novel, Deven, buys the wrath of many only because of his inflinching passion for Urdu poetry. He worships the aged Urdu poet, Noor like anything and keeps pining for his interview to be taped. His one-time college friend, Murad, who fans his frenetic sparks most fraudulently, humbugs Deven in this crazy project. Deven s poetic venture ends in a fiasco and he finds himself all alone. Not only his friend Murad but also the poet, Noor dupe him and Deven is stripped of the entire amount he had managed from the college. He feels himself distanced from his wife, his friend, the poet and society, at large. Deven finds his fate sealed and his future blurred. The last lines of the novel amply demonstrate his anguish:

> He walked up the path. Soon the sun would be up and blazing. The day would begin, with its calamities. They would flash out of the sky and cut him down like swords. He would run to meet them. He ran stopping only to pull a branch of thorns from under his foot.[7]

Anita s *Bye-Bye Blackbird* (1985) runs parallel to Anand s first novel *Untouchable,* as regards the subject matter. Both the novels talk of the problem of discrimination, the biases of caste and creed. While Anand deals with the problem of untouchables, Anita touches upon the problem of black immigrants in England. Both the novels, apart from the historical debate of racial malice and hatred, nurse the sores in the souls of the protagonists.

The novel talks at length about the identity crisis faced by Adit, Sarah and Dev. Adit Sen, a young Indian marries an English girl and settles in England. But after some years, he becomes disillusioned and his humiliation in an alien country creates in him a longing for Indian food and friends. He leaves for India with his English wife, Sarah. His return to India gives birth to Sarah s sorrow. She starts feeling frustrated and her crisis begins. Desai describes her plight most pathetically:

> She had become nameless, she had shed her name as she had shed her ancestry and identity, and she sat there staring as though she watched them disappear. Or

> could only someone who knew her, knew of her background and her marriage, imagine this? Would a stranger have seen in her a lost maiden in search of her name that she seemed, with a silver falling of the light of glamour to an unusually subdued and thoughtful Adit.[8]

In her search for identity, Sarah longs for freedom. It is not a freedom from tradition and conceptions but freedom from the self the self that she wanted to hide.

Anand s Bakha, too in *Untouchable* finding himself trapped and humiliated is full of despair but it is not a moment of defeat. The individual in him rises. He is full of rage. Anand writes:

> The accumulated strength of his giant body glistened in him with the desire for revenge, while horror, rage, indignation swept over his frame.[9]

Mulk Raj Anand, one of the founding fathers of Indian English literature, through his many novels has portrayed Indian life and its conditions at various stages. Dr K.N. Sinha in one of perceptive remarks calls Anand nothing less than a novelist of the human condition, a novelist whose province is human nature. [10] Anand may appear to be a social historian to many but as a novelist, he is not stuck up in his socio-political materials. Gradually, he moves towards a more comprehensive and more assimilative vision of life. Each novel of Anand has several layers of despair and delight. One can hear in his fiction echoes of all kinds. If we look at the evolutionary process, we will modify the conventional perception about his fiction. What Anand told P.K. Rajan philosophically is of great significance:

> I have been evolving a philosophy of the human person which is miscellaneous. It is not doctrinaire thought. It is a number of insights, possibly arising from my experience itself, from all experience. I think we are part of a much bigger universe, we are part of the whole world.[11]

Anand s major novels highlight the individual s fight against society in various forms. His characters become rebels. In addition, this can be traced back in his personal life. Anand rebelled not only against his father but also against all other obstacles to the growth of a free mind, a free spirit. Marlene Fisher finds in Lalu, the protagonist of the second trilogy, and the fictional counterpart of Anand. Lalu symbolizes for Marlene Fisher the natural and spontaneous urge of a new generation to forge his own identity. [12]

Anand s early novels namely *Untouchable, Coolie, Two Leaves and a Bud* deal with the theme of their protagonist s fight to seek their identity. Bakha, the hero of Anand s first novel *Untouchable* (1935) is a victim as an individual of the caste conscious society. The novel describes an inauspicious day in the life of Bakha who s made to feel that he s a sweeper s son and hence untouchable. A well-built child of nature with a stout stature, Bakha feels his agony and wants to react and yet has to restrict himself before his father s subservience to the privileged class. A workaholic Bakha is dutiful and yet the society heaps abuses on him because of his low origin. Wherever he goes, he is belittled with words as defiled and polluted. All these insults and injuries strengthen his body and stiffen his soul. The individual in Bakha even when slapped, does not die but faces only the crisis of identity. E.M. Forster rightly tells:

> Bakha is a real individual, lovable, thwarted sometimes grand, sometimes weak and thoroughly Indian. Even his physique is distinctive; we can recognize his broad intelligent face, graceful torso, and heavy buttocks as he does his nasty jobs, or stumps out in artillery boots in hopes of a pleasant walk through the city with a paper of cheap sweets in his hand.[13]

Besides all pricks and pinches, the novel ends hopefully when Bakha is delighted to know the introduction of a machine, which clears dung and can change the lot of Bakha and his likes. Both the Mahatma and the young poet create in Bakha a new desire to know more about the path to his salvation.

Coolie (1936) deals with the difficulties of Munnoo, the young protagonist who moves from the village to the town, from the town to the city and then to the mountains. A frail boy in a hostile world faces a savage struggle for survival. The novel discusses the sufferings of an individual coolie in a class-ridden society. Munnoo has to endure the foul smell and stink, deep and sticky sweat, dust and heat and dung. His search for delight is menaced by the brutalizing urbanization symbolized by Bombay. In such a climate life is a threat and death is a release. Even in a hostile climate Munnoo s love for the high altitudes does not abate in Bombay. The sudden surge of love and friendship makes the death of Munnoo a memorable and moving moment.

Two Leaves and a Bud (1937) also discusses the theme of exploitation of coolies working in tea garden at the hands of British officials. Gangu, the protagonist of the novel is an old and a beaten man. He is a victim of man, God and civilization. The stifling working conditions make Gangu and his wife sick. His own integrity fails to toe the lines of other coolies who offer their wives or daughters to Reggie Hunt for a piece of land. Gangu s wife dies of cholera and Gangu resigns to his fate. He starts doing a part-time cultivation on a strip of land provided to him through the doctor. But life does not run smooth for Gangu. Once Reggie Hunt s eyes fall on Leila, Gangu s daughter. Hunt wants to defile Leila but Gangu comes in between and is shot. The strain of irony becomes unbearable when Reggie Hunt is discharged. But all these do not signify the end of individual spark. Gangu s zeal and zest for life can be found in the following lines:

> He gripped the handle of his spade with an unwavering faith and dug his foot into the sod made by a furrow and sensed the warm freshness of the earth that would yield fruit.[14]

One can also find a new light in Leila s eyes. The way she bruises the python symbolizes a revolutionary message.

Anand presents Lalu as the hero of his second trilogy. The novels like *The Village, Across the Black Waters* and *The Sword and the Sickle* deal with Lalu s struggle for survival. A young rebel, Lalu is bubbling with energy and vibrating with dreams and determined to reject all the prohibitions and prescriptions of the conservative Indian society. He symbolizes a revolutionary consciousness and a determination to shape his destiny afresh. He joins the war as a professional soldier and his heart bleeds at the sight of death and destruction. The third novel concludes at a note of Lalu s quest for self-realization and self-actualization. He returns to his village, which is still in the grip of dirt, debauchery and disease. Lalu s return is not a defeat but it shows the emerging self of Lalu as an individual against a crippling climate of Indian Society. What brings delight to Lalu is his individual will, which conflicts continuously with the social facts of Indian Life.

The fight between the individual and the society will not be complete if we leave Anand s *The Big Heart, The Road* and *The Death of a Hero*. The protagonists of these novels, experience the severity of all kinds. The fight of the hero in these novels means the conflict between the social reality and the fantasy of the hero. Anant in *The Big Heart* symbolizes the new upsurge in opposition to the old orthodoxy. The novel ends with Anant s death but his death becomes a heroic act of resistance against the orthodoxy. Anant is a big-hearted revolutionary who stands for the redness of heart and not for the blackness of hatred. Anant chooses to die to let others live hopefully and harmoniously. What the poet says after Anant s death is a glowing tribute to the triumphant assertion of Anant s will and spirit:

> One man can die, but life cannot be extinguished in the world altogether until the very sun goes bold and the elements break up.[15]

Bhikhoo in *The Road* and Maqbool in *Death of a Hero* show the same resistance and symbolize a new myth without which nation s resurgence cannot have any meaning.

Anand s women characters are very traditional, confined since he considers them the apostles of love, warmth, and of security *i.e.*, home. But in *The Old Woman and the Cow* (1960), Anand puts in them more voice to oppose their silent sufferings. Gauri, the heroine of the novel becomes conscious of her individual talent and self-esteem and she defies the traditional society and decides to live freely and fearlessly. Gauri s struggle for survival can be viewed as individual s self-discovery and self-actualization. Gauri will not sulk like Narayan s Savitri in *The Dark Room* or Anita Desai s Monisha in *Voices in the City*. She rejects the narrow world of orthodoxy and slams the door against her husband. She does not allow her cultural conditioning to deform her into an image of self-surrender. She does not annihilate her identity. Her life is a pilgrimage of hope and faith, and her inner transformation delights us.

Anand and Anita Desai seem close in voicing their protests against persecution of women in their writings. The women in Anand s early novels seem to bear the brunt under the age-old legacy of man s subordinate being who keep the oven burning to ensure the health and harmony of family in a traditional set-up.

The cause of women s suffering in the early novels of Anand can be ascribed to the lack of education, the blind faith in gods and goddesses and the age old belief of being man s subordinate or secondary. The social taboos appear like mountains in their way to blur their vision (if they had any). Anand portrays them as devoted, docile and dedicated wives but recognizes in them a great potential to pave the path to their progress. The need to allow his women characters to subjugate and to silently suffer the pangs may be traced in Anand s revolutionary fervour. The social reformer in Anand perhaps wanted the women characters to boil and burn as individuals and not as women. Hence, the projection of new women in his later novels is born out of the need to show the other facets of the women. Anand, unlike Anita Desai, allows his women characters to raise their heads to wage war against the system. No doubt, these women characters with their new light of learning want to guard their own fences rather than digging holes in the wall through the sharp nails and hammers of pride and falsity.

Anand s women, like his male protagonists, fight but they also realize the importance of mending walls. The idea of togetherness never skips their mind. One may come across examples where they adjust to the changing times and trends yet for the idea of being one with their husband or lover, they continue the mission even after their counterpart s demise. It is an ample proof of their being individualistic and revolutionary.

The struggle of the individual becomes more potent in Anand s autobiographical novels. Anand adopts the first person narrative in these novels. He shows Krishan, the protagonist of these novels, in conflict with his own emotions and the world, which offers him attractions and distractions. The protagonists loyalty criss-crosses. He disobeys his father. He also breaks the curfew and is sent to jail. He suffers alienations from his father. But even in these moments of despair, he does not leave his quest for truth and his mind is assailed by metaphysical questions like the meaning of life, death and immortality. Krishan has some moments of relaxation in the company of women who give sustenance to his emotional life. *Morning Face* amply demonstrates how personal experience can be transformed to another plane of understanding.

Krishan s struggle for achieving his new identity continues in *Confessions of a Lover*. Once again he is at cross with order and the dictates of society which appear as an impediment between the love of a Hindu boy and a married Muslim woman Yashmin s murder leaves a permanent scar on his soul. But it does not destroy his resistance and zest for life. The journey after Yashmin s death becomes more literal and metaphoric.

Thus, we find that both Anand and Anita deal with the themes of alienation, loneliness, boredom, denial and deprivations of their characters. But the way their characters respond to these major issues is different. Anita s characters in their struggle to find a meaning in life turn inward and become engaged in contemplation, not action. [16]

In order to satisfy their emotional avalanche, they often take the wrong path. Their solitary confinement most often frightens then and they show their reluctance to face reality. However, that does not mean her characters lack vitality and aliveness. In the process of individuation they reveal self-strength and a tendency to emerge out of their isolation, insecurity and anxiety, and gain a closeness and solidarity. [17]

M.R. Anand, on the other hand, offers hope and harmony to his characters in their individual search. The loss of identity in his novels is a moment of despair for his protagonists but he prepares them to regain that identity though after a prolonged struggle. His hero in each novel grows and becomes progressively more sure of himself passing from a low level of consciousness to a more happy adulthood. The inner world of the protagonist in each novel of Anand does not degenerate into a sinister flux. Anand constructs order out of the chaos, strife, confusion and suffering stirs up hope and heroism. For the delight of man according to Radhakrishnan, nothing is to be rejected and everything is to be raised. The empirical man is not sufficient because he dances to the tune of stimuli and is in constant war with the environment. The empirical man has to achieve self-transcendence by exploring new horizons. Man can contend with the disruptive forces and can conquer them. He can emerge from the nervous breakdown. If there is a discord in life, it is only a stage and not the terminus. Life is a continuous pattern of despair and delight and it is not without its dynamic thrust. Man has to make and re-make himself for an authentic living. The nightmare of living in a hostile world brings fear and disquiet for man; but the solitary contemplative sinks again and again into the quiet of self-communion.

M.R. Anand and Anita Desai are the most established novelists in their own right. However, my aim in writing this paper is neither to show the superiority nor inferiority of one above another. The objective of the paper is to show the response of their character to varied situations of life. Both these artists have painted the Indian landscape most dexterously through their characters, situations, dialogues, atmosphere and images. The responses of their characters may be different in the given circumstances but both these novelists portray the dynamic thrust of human personality. The definition of the dynamic thrust of human personality as given by Dr Radhakrishnan can be found in their novels.

> To exist is to stand out of the crowd, to be oneself to be an authentic person making and remaking oneself.[18]

REFERENCES

1. Anita Desai, *Cry the Peacock* (New Delhi: Orient Paperbacks, 1963), 5.
2. Anita Desai, *Voices in the City* (Delhi: Orient Paperbacks, 1965), 48.
3. *Ibid.*, 50.
4. Anita Desai, *Where Shall We Go this Summer* (New Delhi: Orient Paperbacks, 1982), 148.
5. Usha Bande, *The Novels of Anita Desai* (New Delhi: Prestige Books, 1988), 119.

6. William Walsh, *Indian Literature in English* (London and New York: Longman, 1990).
7. Anita Desai, *In Custody* (London: William Heinemann, 1984), 204.
8. Anita Desai, *Bye-Bye Blackbird* (Delhi: Orient Paperbacks, 1985), 31.
9. Mulk Raj Anand, *Untouchable* (New Delhi: Arnold Heinemann, 1935), 57.
10. K.N. Sinha, *M.R. Anand* (New York: Twayne Publishers, World Author Series, 1972).
11. P.K. Rajan, *Studies in M.R. Anand.*
12. Marlene Fisher, Introduction to the *Wisdom of the Heart: A study of the work of M.R. Anand* (New Delhi: Sterling Publishers Pvt. Ltd., 1985).
13. E.M. Forster, Preface to *Untouchable* (New Delhi: Arnold Heinemann, 1984), 9.
14. M.R. Anand, *Two Leaves and a Bud* (New Delhi: Arnold Heinemann, 1983 rpt.), 146.
15. M.R. Anand, *The Big Heart* (New Delhi: Arnold Heinemann, 1980 rpt.), 225.
16. Usha Bande, *The Novels of Anita Desai* (New Delhi: Prestige Books, 1988), 168.
17. *Ibid.*, 172.
18. S.R. Radhakrishnan, *Recovery of Faith* (London: George Allen & Unwin), 95.

9

Anand s Vision of War and Death in *Across the Black Waters*

D. RAMAKRISHNA

Despite the tendency of scholars to treat Mulk Raj Anand as a writer concerned only with the rustics and the downtrodden, there are several other facets of his genius like art and cross-cultural studies. Coming after *Untouchable* (1933), *Across the Black Waters* (1940) deals with the larger human concerns of war and death in the context of the protagonist s encounter with the Western culture. Read in the light of modern war literature, Anand s fictional rendering of World War I is amazingly refreshing, in spite of the rusticity of the characters involved.

As the second of the Lalu trilogy, *Across the Black Waters* follows *The Village* (1939) which ends with Lalu s joining the Indian sepoys bound for Vilayat (England). As Anand tells us before the opening of the novel, he wrote the first draft of *Across the Black Waters* in Barcelona, Madrid during January and April 1937 and rewrote it at Chinnor, Oxfordshire between July and December 1939. The novel was based on the author s impressions of the Spanish Civil War as well as his own imagination or recollections of those who fought in Flanders. In a recent interview to *The New Indian Express*, Anand says: I spent several months at Flanders to get the feel of the situation and only then did I embark on writing the book. [1] As many as 1200 of the British Indian army went to Flanders and only 50 of them came back after the War was over. Hence, he says, I wanted to bring out the pathos. [2] Translated into eleven European languages, the novel has recently been adapted by the British Council into a play to mark the

80th anniversary of the end of World War I. The play travelled all over England and a seminar on the novel was held in Birmingham.

Whereas in *Untouchable* and other novels dealing with the social theme Anand is concerned with suffering inflicted on the downtrodden, in *Across the Black Waters* he deals with the humanistic theme in respect to the ruthless destruction of man by man with the machine. The pity of it is the soldiers, whether rustic or otherwise, are generally those joining the army to win bread for their families.

Referring to Lal Singh, K.R. Srinivasa Iyengar says: His heart beats in response to the primordial life of the village, but his mind incessantly rebels and yearns for the dim, distant, alluring horizons. [3] In fact, it is not for any such idealistic concerns that Lal Singh goes out of his village Nandpur but as an escape from the vicious climate around, as an act of desperation. This, of course, is a blessing in disguise for him since the full potential in him emerges and he could achieve self-realization in his encounters abroad. Towards the end of *Across the Black Waters,* Lalu reflects on fate, reminiscing his life in Nandpur culminating in his narrow escape: And then the landlord and the police had come up with a warrant for his arrest on a trumped up charge and he ran away [...]. The only escape from prison was to join the army. [4] The self-realization or growth of the adolescent hero is, in fact, his struggle for survival. Lal Singh s defiant nature is evident from the fact that he as a Sikh cuts his hair and registers as a Dogra. While he was helpless back home, he has his ultimate revenge on the foreign soil, as fate would have it. This is what Anand calls Kismet (299). Lalu has to play out his destined role and grow into full manhood, defying even death. It is not the situation of a mercenary for money alone to pay off debts to the landlord. It is destiny that elevates to heroism the otherwise nondescript individual, bringing him laurels; and his adversaries stand exposed in all their small-mindedness. As Alastair Niven says, Anand s overriding concern in *Across the Black Waters,* almost the sole preoccupation of the novel, is with the devastating effect of war upon the individual. [5] Anand s clear message on the individual level in respect to the protagonist is that the course of destiny cannot be changed by the mighty. While the powerful landlord and the police stand reduced to insignificance, Lal Singh emerges as a war hero abroad. Even on the front, of course, he has to face petty jealousies and prejudices like those of Subah who tries to get Lalu court-martialed but makes a fool of himself due to the sagacity of Ajitan Sahib.

Lalu and the other sepoys, even though bound ostensibly for Vilayat (England), find their ship docking in French waters. For Lalu, surviving the voyage across the ocean with its deep blue ("black") waters is a matter for thanks giving to the Heavens:

> 'So we have come across the black waters safely,' he said to himself apprehensively, as if he really expected some calamity, the legendary fate of all those who went beyond the seas, to befall him at any moment. Truly, the black, or rather blue, water seemed uncanny, spreading for thousands of miles. (8)

To the superstitious rustics, the "blackness" of the sea waters is associated with death because the voyage is into the realm of the Unknown.

In "Eagles and Pigeons," Mustafa survives the shipwreck confronting a situation Lalu refers to as the "legendary fate of all those who went beyond the seas." As Mustafa says,

> I always laughed at the Mullah for saying everything was ordained by God, and mocked at my mother for believing in Fate, and I still don't believe in either, but I tell you one thing—the moment when Life meets Death is frightening.[6]

It is this point of Life meeting Death that causes the grimness of the novel *Across the Black Waters.* In the midst of the combat with the rising tension among the soldiers and heart-burn caused by the conflict with the officers, "They had no hope or faith in their hearts except the fate to which they had resigned themselves, their Kismet, which, more and more, had begun to look like the premonition of a horrible death" (251). The soldiers experience comeraderie in the face of a common doom going to befall soon. In the midst of the gun fire, the sepoys seem to be engaged in a quest, sitting "patient and tranquil though rather pale and silent, as if they were reflecting on their doom [...] each to his own, as if everyone were alone in this ordeal (142). As J. Glenn Gray says in *The Warriors*:

> [...] the soldier who has yielded himself to the fortunes of war, has sought to kill and to escape, being killed, or who has even lived long enough in the disordered landscape of battle, is no longer what he was [...]. His moods and disposition are affected by the presence of others and the encompassing environment of threat and fear [...].[7]

Lalu and companions on the front are involved in such a situation. They are faced with the mounting fear caused by the army machine which works with the ponderous efficiency of a force which had, for the time being, ground out all individual considerations (233). Anand s vision of war reminds us of what Simone Weill says:

> As soon as the practice of war has revealed the fact that each moment holds the possibility of death, the mind becomes incapable of moving from one day to the next day without passing through the spectre of death [...].[8]

In dealing with the plight of the Indian sepoys in Flanders in 1914, Anand seems to be making a universal statement concerning the nature of war. His description of the appalling brutalities of war on account of his deep compassion for human suffering reminds us of the rendition of the effects of war by poets like Wilfred Owen, Siegfried Sassoon, and David Jones. Like the English poets, Anand too successfully evokes the pity of war and the poetry that is in the pity.

As the regiment of the Indian sepoys starts marching towards the battle front, the novelist reflects on the insanity of war:

> The element of sanity in Lalu persisted in the face of guns and in the face of the insanity which had blown off the towers of the churches, and he could not believe that ordinary men and women of good sense, and the Governments of France, England and Germany, which were saner and wiser than the ordinary people over whom they ruled, could be engaged in a war in which

> men were being killed and wounded and houses shattered. (92-93)

Kirpu feels that even the rats in the sahibs houses seem shrewd and wonders why such rich people are killing each other and making a large graveyard of this land (197). Bishop Padre, who visits the soldiers in the midst of the war, says it is a holy war (309). When Lalu observes the bonhomie among the enemies, the British and German soldiers, on Christmas day, he wonders at the mockery of war (303).

Across the Black Waters has a cultural dimension presented through interaction among the Indian sepoys and their general reaction to the British officers. Of course, heroism and the use of the machine on the front may cross all cultural barriers since the soldiers go desperate in the face of the death. Initially, on arrival at the French port and marching through the streets of Marseilles, the Indian soldiers with their rustic backgrounds experience culture shock. The scarcely clad French girls, the public hugging and kissing of men and women, the dancing couples and the pleasures of Vilayat are the initial surprises to the Indian soldiers. Anand comments on the class difference between the British and Indian officers (38), the Angrezi and the Indians, the sahibs and sepoys. There are divisions among the sepoys too the sneaks, the shirkers, and the twisters. There is greater discipline on the part of the British officers and warmer officer-soldier relationship. The Indian sepoys are generally loyal to the British: We have eaten the salt, Daddy Dhanoo says, It is a question of gratitude (137). Despite the Indian soldiers amazement at the glitter abroad, there is a sense of the superior on their part. Daddy Dhanoo says with decision: They have no religion. No law, They drink wine and make eyes at women. They believe in this life only. Eat, drink, shit! (73).

Lalu s own reaction to these things around him is one of emptiness from the centre of which his two eyes seemed to see this world as an enormous enclosure, crowded by hordes of hard, gigantic shapes which were oppressing him (56). This sense of loneliness has been in the very nature of the youth from his days at Nandpur. On looking at the statue of Joan of Arc, Lalu is reminded of Rani of Jhansi and feels the blood coursing in his veins with the ambition to follow her on the path of glory (41). In fact, Lalu as the centre of all conflict, is in the process of a movement from war within to war without. For him the confrontation now is not with social forces but elemental forces.

While in the trenches, the boy Lalu is frightened like a baby (188). Seeing bayonet attacks on the battlefield, he is reminded of the oxen butchered by the village cobbler. He trembles like the school boy, the dread loomed before his eyes (142). On seeing the train of wounded soldiers, Lalu swoons: A sudden tremor of dread spread like a panic in his brain [...]. It seemed unending, this torturous journey into the Unknown (78-79). He feels: if one who slays one is a murderer than he who slays a thousand is not a hero (137). Referring to modern terror caused by the World War, Frederick J. Hoffman says: The word *murder* no longer has any meaning in a situation permitting a mass production of corpses. [9] Lalu suffers a conflict within himself:

> In him the two poles of nature seemed always to have been quarrelling, as if he had not decided whether to burst out of his skin, as it were, and live outside himself, or to recline back, self-exiled, pain-marred, mutilated with the memories of those hindrances which the world had put in his way. The two anti-types had revolved in a furious whirl of the axle tree during his boyhood. He was the contradiction who had cultivated a pride in excess of a dignity, even as he had gone carelessly about, playing pranks with the boys of his village and laughing at the grey beards, bent on the consummation of his unrestricted impulses, as if he could cheat nature and take happiness by surprise. (277)

The deaths of Daddy Dhanoo, Lakhman Singh and Uncle Kirpu intensely agitate Lalu and with his ego looming larger and larger, he says, So, after all, Iam in for it (280).

Alastair Niven says that Lalu and the sepoys are rustics, unsuited to modern warfare, are herded by the thousand to fight in Europe for the King Emperor. [10] The Indian soldiers do fight despite their rusticity once they are on the front. Whatever the cultural background of the soldier, he has no identity. As Frederick J. Hoffman rightly observes, the soldier is unknown, existing in a state of unreality, anonymity. [11] In this connection, it is interesting to compare Anand s *Across the Black Waters* with Stephen Crane s *The Red Badge of Courage* (1895). Henry Fleming, the protagonist in Crane s novel, is generally called the youth, or he, and he is an inexperienced soldier, an unknown quantity, torn between a little panic-fear and visions of broken-bladed glory as he faces his first battle in the Civil War. Determined to be a hero, Fleming suddenly turns coward. He then recovers and behaves as the fighter he had wished to be. In both the novels the theme is that man s salvation lies in change and spiritual growth. It is only by immersion in the flux of experience that man becomes disciplined or develops in character, conscience or soul. Whatever the intensity of fear presented in the novels in the face of combat, it is the self-combat of the youth who fears and initially resists change and spiritual growth. Fleming fearlessly plunges into battle, charging the enemy like a pagan who defends his religion. [12]

As a typical War novel, *Across the Black Waters* has in its texture the theme of not only death but also of love. One of the greatest American War novels, Ernest Hemingway s *For Whom the Bell Tolls* (1940) depicts the hero Robert Jordan s love for Maria in the midst of war. Having planned a trilogy, Anand was obviously anxious to bring his hero Lal Singh back to India for the third novel, *The Sword and the Sickle* (1942). If he allowed Lalu to die on the battlefield as his final noble act of sacrifice in the context of the deaths of his dear friends, Anand s novel would have achieved the poignancy of Hemingway s novel, which resulted from the American author s journalistic adventures in the Spanish Civil War. Some of the deeper strengths of Hemingway s novel come from his long involvement with Spain, as Carlos Baker tells us.[13] Interestingly, Anand s War novel too was based upon his personal experiences in Spain. Robert Jordan s story acquires its poignancy from the fact that he is guided by the conviction that man s chief duty is to do everything he can do for collective human dignity and freedom and that it is the individual s chief obligation of sacrifice himself for the human community which is his greatest opportunity for a transcendent act. As Jordan says, fatally wounded and lying on the hillside almost delirious, "I have fought for what I believed in for a year now. If we win here we will win everywhere. The world is a fine place and worth the fighting for [...]."[14] Jordan has the choice between love and duty before the bridge-blowing. The bliss of his love for Maria is the great compensation for the inevitability of catastrophe. However, his sense of duty obliterates anything else. In Anand's novel *Across the Black Waters* too love is the only refuge in the midst of the unmitigated horrors of war and forebodings of death. Lalu, having been "the dehumanized toy of destiny," and "in the face of the unknown, in full view of the spectacle of destruction and death," yields to the "strange purblind tenderness of love" (239). As Uncle Kirpu says, "love is to escape from this beastliness" of war (241-43). Ever since Lalu sees Marie, as he and the other sepoys are playing on the bank of the stream, he has been fascinated by her looks, and "she seemed to have wrought some magic on Lalu" (224). The innocence and beauty of the girl, in contrast to the ferocity of the war, greatly fascinate him, "his head surcharged with madness" (225). On account of his love for Marie, Lalu has to face the jealousy of Subah Singh who tries to get Lalu court-martialed. Notwithstanding these things, Lalu has to march forward on the battlefield: "Abjectly grateful for the smaller mercies of life, he sought to crush the luxury of desire and went about like the dehumanized toy of destiny, which was the unknown will of the Sarkar" (239). Henceforward he plunges into the battle, prepared for annihilation as per the will of the Unknown Sarkar above, the ultimate destiny that governs human life: "Lalu felt intoxicated by the urge to get to the crest and ran forward blindly" (321). Wounded by a bullet that has pierced through the calf of his left leg, he falls, face forward. By the time he opens his eyes, he finds himself being dragged by a German soldier, and "He resigned himself to the mercy of his captors" (322).

Anand has successfully evoked the atmosphere of war in which the Indian sepoys fight alongside the British in a magnificent display of bravery and loyalty. The masterful depiction of the combat on the front in *Across the Black Waters* and Ernest Hemingway. The unknown rustic Indian soldier displays the courage and conviction equal to that of any Western war hero. It is at these levels that Anand achieves universalization of presenting the horrors of war as well as the pity that it evokes.

NOTES

1. Vinita Deshmukh, Going Global from Khandala, *The New Indian Express,* January 24, 1999.
2. *Ibid.*
3. K.R. Srinivasa Iyengar, *Indian Writing in English* (New Delhi: Sterling Publishers Pvt. Ltd., 1962), 347.
4. Mulk Raj Anand, *Across the Black Waters* (1949; Delhi: Orient Paperbacks, 1980), 301. Hereafter page references to this edition are given in parentheses.
5. Alastair Niven, *The Yoke of Pity: A Study in the Fictional Writings of Mulk Raj Anand* (New Delhi: Arnold-Heinemann, 1978), 71.
6. Mulk Raj Anand, Eagles and Pigeons, *The Barber□s Trade Union and Other Stories* (London: Jonathan Cape, 1944), 171.
7. J. Glenn Gray, *The Warriors* (New York: Harcourt, Brace, 1959), 27.
8. Simon Weill, The Iliad Poem of Might, Intimations of Christianity, tr. Elizabeth C. Geissbuhler (Boston: Beacon Press, 1958), 41.
9. Frederick J. Hoffman, *The Mortal No: Death and the Modern Imagination* (Princeton: Princeton University Press, 1964), 269.
10. Alastair Niven, 68.
11. Frederick J. Hoffman, 15.
12. Stephen Crane, *The Red Badge of Courage* (1894; New York: The Modern Library, 1951), 194-95.
13. Carlos Baker, *Ernest Hemingway: A Life Story* (New York: Scribner s, 1969), 302-30; 345-48.
14. Ernest Hemingway, *For Whom the Bell Tolls* (New York: Scribner s, 1940), 502.

10

MULK RAJ ANAND S *UNTOUCHABLE*: A SOCIAL DOCUMENT

T.M.J. INDRA MOHAN

A colossus in the Indian novel in English, Mulk Raj Anand occupies a pride of place among the Indian novelists by occupying himself historically the two worlds: one the colonial decades and the other post-colonial generations. A committed humanist believes in the amelioration of society on the socialist principles with which he thinks that heaven on earth is possible. Anand felt that imagination is infinite. It produces Hamlet, Lear and Othello as well as Heer and Ranjha. As a writer according to Anand, has to see the relation of the concrete with the universal.

Mulk Raj Anand s love for humanity and his concern for the socially and economically oppressed came from his peasant mother and father who was a traditional copper smith. In consequence Anand acquired a status of being the advocate of the downtrodden and the underprivileged. His novels are explosive sometimes because he openly expressed in a vehement way certain social maladies in his writings.

Anand came to limelight with the publication of his first novel *Untouchable* in 1935. He felt that only by exercising the inherent artistic gift in the right direction one could achieve greatness and he made the attempt with full vigour towards the set goal in which he became successful.

The novel was the result of the vanity of youth wanting recognition, the departure from absolute philosophical theories towards a search for philosophical insights based on the lives of the human beings whom one knew in the flesh and blood, the urge to express oneself at all costs in an absolutist manner so as to expose the ugliness of death in life by deliberately dramatising even through distortion, the non-human realities which impinged on one from all sides (*Critical Essays on Indian Writing in English* 6). Anand s *Untouchable* is a focus on class distinctions between the rich and the poor, between the tea planters and labourers, between the high caste Hindus and the dregs of humanity, known as untouchables hamper the growth of individuals which ultimately result in social evils. He hated the social institution which cause the cleavage between the different strata in the social structure. He presents simple and noble human beings enmeshed in the net of poverty and injustice. Though they fight to come out of it they are helpless to shake off the coils of social evil.

The novel *Untouchable* covers the events of a single day in the life of a low caste boy Bakha, in the town of Bulashah. The eighteen-year-old boy is one of the sons of Lakha, the jemedar of the sweepers of the town. Bakha is the child of the 20th century. He comes under the influences of the modern world which cause stirrings within him. From a Tommy he has secured a pair of old breeches and from a sepoy a pair of old boots. At the dawn of every day he begins his work of latrine cleaning and he thinks that he is an efficient worker. His sister Sohini faces the onslaught of the upper class people in the area when she approaches the well to get water. She tells her father they think we are dirt because we clean their dirt. Similarly her brother faces the wrath of the upper class people when Bakha lifts the boy who is injured in a hockey game. The boy s mother yells at him saying that he has polluted her son by touching him and lifting him from the ground. Now Bakha understands twin problems of caste and poverty squalor and backwardness.

As suggested by Mahatma Gandhi, Anand had made certain changes in the novel *Untouchable.* Anand s life and experience in Sabarmati Ashram proved in realising the characters in the novel. The periods of meditation in the Ashram helped Anand to recollect the social structure of India where the downtrodden were made to suffer because of their birth and station in life. His recollection and Gandhiji s preachings to show devotion to the poor was a strong source of conversion for Anand. He began to realise in his mind to create an oppressed character caught in the villainy of the Indian social structure subjecting them to untold suffering and humiliation. The result was the creation Bakha in *Untouchable.* The intense and passionate feelings of Anand for the oppressed comes to the fore in the novel. It is a sensitive subject which Anand has taken up to deal with in the novel. Though it has been more than half a century hence the social evil has not died down nor has it been completely wiped out in India. Anand is the harbinger to focus the social onslaught in absolute realistic terms in his novel *Untouchable.*

Anand is a committed writer to the social cause. His penetrating thought and humane attitude in understanding the grim social realities in India found their expression in his novel. *Untouchable* is a revolutionary novel of protest against the pervading social evil in India. Anand s social awareness and objective impelled him to create the novel to focus the social evil and to rally for the removal of the social evil by inculcating in the minds of the Indian intellectuals to put their mite to end the social evils once for all. In a significant manner that Anand s novel *Untouchable* was published at a time when social reformers in India were engaged in an earnest way to remove casteism and untouchability.

The privileged caste Hindus in India has caused mental depression to the untouchables, we find this in Bakha s agonised interrogation What have I done to deserve all this ? (*Untouchable* 133). Anand took it upon himself as a social critic and wanted to bring the atrocities perpetuated upon the untouchables to light. He often uses irony as a form to expose the social evils. One of the well-known critics on the works of Anand, Saros Cowasjee s observations in *So Many Freedoms* is worth quoting here: As irony is implicit in the theme, one finds it everywhere more pervasively than in any other Anand s novel. The novel unfolds with the child of modern India, shackled by age old tradition; the Hindus who pride themselves on their cleanliness gargle and the spit in the stream and pollute the water while a person incomparably cleaner than themselves is treated like dirt. The precise situation permeated the Indian social order with divisions based on communities and the work that each community takes up for the sake of food and survival in the late 19th century and in the subsequent century also without any change (55).

Anand s commitment to reveal the deep-rooted social malice in the Indian society made him to create Bakha. He had wanted to show the youth s unique sensitiveness as against the people of the upper caste who thought merely touching him is a degradation (Conversations with Anand). He further narrated that I meant symbolically to show that such small tenderness among people in private life or the catharsis of human existence (Conversations).

Bakha arrests our attention in the entire novel. As E.M. Forster observes that Bakha is a real individual, lovable, thwarted, sometimes grand, sometimes weak, and thoroughly Indian. Even his physique is distinctive, we can recognise broad intelligent face, graceful torso [...] as he does is nasty job or stumps out in artillery boots, in the hope of a pleasant walk through the city with a paper of cheap sweets in his hands (Preface to *Untouchable* 9). Anand with his remarkable skill portrays Bakha s helplessness, frustration, anxiety and agony to the degree that he has become an embodiment of his own creation or in other words the creator and the creator co-mingle at one point.

Dr Radhakrishnan observes that The institution of caste illustrates the spirit of comprehensive synthesis characteristic of the Hindu mind with its faith in the collaboration of races and the co-operation of cultures. Paradoxically as it may seem, the system of caste is the outcome of tolerance and trust. Though it has now degenerated into an oppression and intolerance, though it tends to perpetuate inequality and develop the spirit of exclusiveness these unfortunate effects are not the central motives of the system (*The Hindu View of Life*, Unwin Books, 1963: 67). The casteism becomes a pivotal issue in the Indian society and it crosses the point of tolerance as evidenced in *Untouchable*.

The temple episode in the *Untouchable* throw light on the sad plight of the outcastes. They were not allowed to enter the portals of temples because their contact would defile the house of God, the creator of all. Lakha, Bakha s father, wanted to keep himself at home under the pretext of sickness and entrusted the work of cleaning the roads and the temples in the town to Bakha. After the excruciating experience of touching in the market, Bakha went to sweep the temple courtyard. He was filled with the fear of some unknown and mysterious effect on him as he entered the courtyard of the temple.

Bakha surveyed the heap of dust and leaves which he had come to clear. He threw the basket and the broom on the ground and was ready to begin his job. He saw a miniature temple with the beautifully polished image of a snake enclosed. He was slightly afraid of the snake but his fear ceased when he saw the devotees worshipping it. He shouted his call of caution to avoid the repetition of the disaster of the morning. The orthodox crowd of worshippers was conscious of his evil presence. He was in a fix and did not know what those people worshipped there. He heard the worshippers chanting Ram, Ram, Sri, Hari, Narayan, Sri Krishna, Hey Hanuman jodha, Kali Mai. He had faint idea about some of them and did not know anything about the rest. He was obsessed with the desire of seeing the images of gods and goddesses. But he had not courage to go up. He knew that an untouchable going into a temple polluted it past purification.

As his curiosity became more and more acute, he dismissed his conflicting thoughts and moved towards the stairs. Looking here and there he climbed up a few stairs but soon fear returned and he came back to the place from which he had started. Describing his condition Dr Anand writes, He became the humble oppressed underdog that he was by birth, afraid of everything creeping slowly up, in a curiously hesitant, cringing movement. With his broom he began to collect the litter. It was a slow business but not so wearying and unpleasant as that of working at the latrines.

Again his curiosity propelled him to go up the stairs. He strengthened himself and climbed up a few more stairs and from a safe distance he saw the spectacle of the worshippers, priests and the sanctuary which had so far been a secret, a hidden mystery to him. He was wonderstruck at the sight of beautiful brass images. Bakha saw that the morning service had begun. Devout worshippers stood singing Arti in a chorus. Bakha was profoundly moved by the song. He unconsciously joined his hands in the worship of the unknown god.

All of a sudden he heard a loud cry polluted, polluted, polluted. He was perplexed. He knew what is meant. He saw a little man a priest of the temple, stumbling, falling and crying, polluted, polluted, polluted. He also saw the figure of a woman Sohini, behind the shouting priest. The crowd of devotees began to run helter-skelter. All of them were in a terrible orgy of excitement. One of them angrily shouted at Bakha and charged him of defiling their whole service. Bakha ran down the steps and went to his sister Sohini. The little priest was angrily shrieking, You people have only been polluted from a distance. I have been defiled by contact. The crowd felt that the priest had suffered terribly. All worshippers sympathized with him but they did not ask about the way he had been polluted.

Anand concludes the novel *Untouchable* with a note of faith and idealism. As Bakha returns home his mind is raised with the hope that soon the flush system would come then the sweepers can be free from the stigma of untouchability and assume the dignity of status that is their right as useful members of a casteless and classless society (173). The manifest plea in the novel is for the total abolition of untouchability. Bakha fervently hopes for the dawn to his nature of his work and his relevance in the society without the label of untouchable.

The novel *Untouchable* acquires human significance and social relevance when Anand meticulously brings out the inner life of Bakha. It was a growing concern for metaphoric untouchables in all cultures and walks of life. Anand also brings to focus Bakha s smouldering rage. His feelings are compared to spurts of smoke from a self smothered fire. His unspoken words are described as the soundless speech of cells receiving and transmitting the emotions, which one day would spit fire that is what Anand felt probably when he wrote the novel. The novelist wants humane gestures towards the underprivileged like Bakha. The novel s cleanness of structure celebrates un-cleanness not so much of Bakha s work as of the minds and sensibilities of those among whom he lives. The cheap minded temple priest and the cruel townsmen and the malicious gossiping women with their assumed superior upper castedness are in striking contrast to Bakha. It is not Bakha who pollutes them so much as it is their own fear of being polluted, a fear that destroys to see the realities. The fear also dehumanises them.

The inhuman treatment meted out to Bakha in *Untouchable* could have really happened to a social outcaste during the colonial days in India, perhaps such cruelties are being perpetuated in many parts of villages even today which the objective newspapers publish. Undoubtedly, Anand had drawn upon what he had himself witnessed and heard as a boy, he brings into print in the form of a novel. As a novelist addressing himself to the task of exposing social evils, Anand has been an effective writer and he can be compared to Dickens in this respect. The novel evokes in the mind of the objective reader, the horrifying social malady that existed in the colonial days and in the subsequent decades makes a tale of socially created woe to the downtrodden in the Indian society. Perverted orthodoxy in the name of religion and the deadness of human feeling become the twin evils which systematically destroy any effort made by the government and the social organisations to eradicate the untouchability in the society.

Anand s down-to-earth portrayal of the naked realities of our social evils which are dismal and harrowing, makes *Untouchable* a social document besides being a novel first of its kind in the colonial Indian social context. Despite the legal protection offered to the untouchables in the Indian society, even now when such inhuman incidents are reported in the Indian dailies we are compelled to think the past social maladies still continue in some parts of our nation. Hence Anand s *Untouchable* is relevant even today and if social evils are not eradicated completely in India, probably this novel all the more would become significant to the present and posterity, as a pathetic social document.

REFERENCES

Anand, Mulk Raj. *Untouchable*, New Delhi: Arnold Heinemann, 1984.

Cowasjee, Saros. *So Many Freedoms: A Study of the Major Fiction of Mulk Raj Anand*, New Delhi: Oxford University Press, 1977, 55.

Forster, E.M. *Preface to Untouchables*, New Delhi: Arnold Heinemann, 1984, 9.

Taped Conversations with Anand, Bombay, May 17, 1973.

11

Two Leaves and a Bud: A Proletariat Novel

N.P. RAVI KUMAR

Mulk Raj Anand is one of the prominent figures in the colonial and the post-colonial Indian writing in English. His novels reveal a blend of idealism, socialism and a keen perception of the contemporary social issues. His characters long for a meaning in their living and a search for their identity. The *Two Leaves and a Bud* may be said to be essentially, a dramatic novel. It culminates in a tragic clash of interest and destinies. This novel may be said to be an extension of *Coolie*. Gangu, the hero of the novel is an improved version of Munoo.

The story is set in north-western part of India. He crosses India from a village near Hoshiarpur in the Punjab to the Macpherson Tea estate in distant Assam. He takes with him his wife Sajani and his children Leila and Buddhu. The tea plantation is a world within a world. The coolie Narayan tells Gangu: I suppose it was in our kismet. But at home it was like a prison, and here it is slightly worse [...]. First water, afterwards mire! This prison has no bars but it nevertheless an unbreakable jail. The chowkidars keep guard over the plantation, and they bring you back if you should run [...]. The foreign investors exploit the masses. Still worse is the Indian sardars also equally exploit the masses here. But there are good Britishers like Dr John who wants to show human consideration and fellow feeling. He used to remark often it is the country we have no right to do it. There is Croft-Cooke the boss of the plantation and his wife is highly reasonable with regard to the plantation labourers. The villain of the novel is Reggie Hunt, the assistant manager who is known for his cruelty and lust. Gangu has unwittingly walked into his trap. With all his innocence he thought that Hunt would be an honest manager. Gangu thinks that he has played into the hands of the unscrupulous people. He wanted to do hard work at the same time remain honest.

Anand brings in the pathetic condition of labourers working in the plantation. The dreadful malaria breaks out and Gangu s wife Sajani dies. Discontent gathers volume like a boil and chance collision makes it burst. When two women quarrel in the plantation Hunt behaves like a brute and some coolies are injured. An appeal is made to Croft who disregards their appeal. The coolies decide to demonstrate but division arises between the coolies. One group wants to demonstrate and the other group does not want to participate. Dr John who has sympathy for the plantation workers is summarily dismissed and leaves the scene for good. Hunt is hated by coolies and to an extent by the white community also. He approaches Leila with an ulterior motive when she is alone and she runs away. Urged by the mad lust and maddened by frustration and fear he shoots, in which Gangu is killed. A trail follows and in the judgment Hunt is declared not guilty.

The painful truth of the living condition of the labourers in the plantation is told in a gripping manner. According to Goronwyree great skill and without insistence the Indian Coolies, exploited starving cheated dirty diseased as a true heirs of the world s great civilizations (*The Spectator*, April 1937: 382). There were angry protests between The Spectator and Mulk Raj Anand Encouraged by Ree s Review, Anand wrote in *The Spectator*, June 11, 1937 that he had exposed the prevailing conditions of the labourers working in the tea plantation. However Mr Godwin, owner of a tea estate in Assam challenged Anand s view in the 20th August 1937 issue of the story in *The Spectator*. Strangely Whitley who chaired the royal commission of labourers had recommended the British Planters for their human treatment of labourers working in the plantations. Again Anand gave a rejoinder in the magazine on 3rd September 1937 stating that Whitley report was far from the truth. But somehow the Britishers had the impression that the Indian labourers were lazy, liars and sub-human creatures. The sordid picture of the life of the labourers in the plantation somehow did not catch the attention of the rulers. To add to their woe, the Indian capitalist were also equally responsible for the sorry plight of the labourers. They were orphaned by the Indian society itself.

Anand is reported to have the facts on the spot after a meeting with Gandhi at Sabarmati. He attacks social snobbery and social prejudice. For him the novel should change the life of the masses. He felt that the true creative ability if it put into reality should transform the society. People should strive for a change to better their living condition. His idea is that subservient mind of the masses is responsible for their own degradation. Anand displays a mature sense of writing with an objective to bring in transformation in the sleepy Indian society. He does not want meek submission to unwanted authoritarinism. The capitalist forces would take advantage of the social disintegration of the masses. That is what precisely happens in *Two Leaves and a Bud*. The injustice having been perpetuated systematically and legally by the British rulers when Gangu was killed was due to the mass disarray in the society. For a daylight murder the culprit escapes casually without even reprimand with the blessings of the judges.

The Britisher in the novel John is an ideal character which Anand has created in order to infuse some sense in the British rulers. When Gangu requests him to make recommendation to the English boss for land he tells Gangu Yes I will do that. Certainly you ought to get land; it is in the contract of every labourer that you will have land to grow rice on when he comes here. I will see that the contract is enforced (133). No one will believe that the Britisher would speak such a plain and honest language to an insignificant coolie. It is obvious that Anand had created the Britisher with the sole aim of exposing the crime against the labourers committed by the foreign capitalist. Gangu being innocent takes for granted that he would get automatically one day a piece of land for himself. But to his rude shock he comes to know from Narain that the labourers can get land if only they send their daughters or wives to the estate owners. Through Narain the author shows what kind of life the labourers lead in the plantation.

Anand s *Two Leaves and a Bud* is the result of his first-hand knowledge of the living condition of the labourers. According to H.C. Harrex that Anand s characterisations within the proletarian campus are strong varied and impassioned [...] his social criticism is usually spirited and challenging (*The Fire and the Offering* 144). His humanitarian protest and his desire to uplift the life of downtrodden from their degradation, he felt that it was his mission in life. He has risen above sectarian or communal outlook and consistently wrote and spoke against capitalists and pleaded for the cause of the downtrodden. Anand s objective is humanistic but sometimes his approach is vehement and passionate. He does not believe in harrowing conditions with which the labourers live as their fate. He is rational in his approach. He believes that one day the suffering would come to an end but to make the process they have to rise.

This novel is a record of his concern for the oppressed coolies on the Tea Estates managed by the British. Poetic in style, this novel presents the pathetic life of the coolies of Assam Tea Estates. A fierce denunciation of man s cruelty to man, *Two Leaves and a Bud* projects Anand s humanism, his rejection of his theories of Karma and God and the destructive effects of poverty and fatalism. Anand was almost blind with rage at the cruelty inflicted on the coolies by the English capitalists and their Indian jockeys. The events in the novel are narrated in a well structured manner. The coolies are over worked and underpaid. Their living condition is inhuman. Sajani catches malaria and dies. Gangu approaches Mr Croft for a loan to perform the last rites. He kicks out Gangu. The disappointed Gangu seeks the help of Buta, who is equally helpless.

The calm atmosphere of the estate is rudely disturbed by the quarrel between two coolie-women. Ruggie rushes to the spot and beats up the labourers. The labourers rush to house of Dr Harve who is totally taken aback by the reaction of the labourers. He attends to them, and advises them to see the Burya Shaib and seek his help in getting justice. The mentally and physically broken coolies are too weak to protest. During their gathering at Narain s house they learn about the futility of their attempt. The coolies learn that those who attempted to run away from the estate in the past were to put to death.

The Royal Air Force planes are summoned to instill a sense of fear in the minds of coolies. Dr Harve is also dismissed. Miss Barbara deserts the doctor and is pleased to remain with her parents. The tiger shoot is a stage managed one. Reggie who is always with a list wants to have Leila. He approaches her when she is alone plucking tea. Being threatened she runs for her safety. Frustrated he shoots, in the melee Gangu is fatally wounded.

The trial of Reggie lasts for three days, and jury acquit him of all charges. Pertinently K.R. Srinivasa Iyengar comments: *Two Leaves And A Bud* may be said to be essentially a dramatic novel, and certainly it culminates in a tragic clash of interests and destinies and what is fine is put out, and what is dark is triumphant (*Indian Writing in English* 343).

The labourers are treated with contempt. There is no union among the labourers to expose their cause. The labourers are kept almost in a quarantine. They are prevented from conversing with each other. They were forced to live in filth. The impact of western culture interfered with the traditional patterns of living. Deprived of their roots the labourers had to suffer. The Coolies were trapped and brought here. They came with a fond hope of getting something for their survival. Srinivasa Iyengar says: Superficially, the foreign exploiters and the masses of the exploited (the collies) make the main pattern of tension in the novel. But quite a few of the Indians the sardars, the mistris, the babus the warders are exploiters too, and between them create an atmosphere of twisting and turning for the coolies. On the other hand, there are also the good idealistic Britishers [ ] (*Indian Writing in English* 344).

Mrs Croft brands the natives as Lie-Box. The poor coolies under the stress of penury are silent. Poverty paralyses them. It is ironical to note that while the poor labour class are toiling hard, their masters waste their time over a cup of tea discussing the weather condition oblivious of the living condition of the poor. The Britishers maintain their superiority over the Coolies by their lavish dress and they sent shock and fear to the coolies. They carefully guarded their polo grounds and houses while black coolies were left to fend for themselves. The privileged class violated the human rights of the poor.

This novel brought to light the inhuman cruelty perpetrated by the whites. Anand felt so outraged at this inhuman treatment that he painted the exploiters in the darkest hue and in consequence the British Government had banned this book.

Anand inaugurated a new era in the Indo-Anglican literature by choosing to depict the pathetic plight of the poor and underdogs. He rejects fate and points out that all these are man made and the result of the meekness of the masses. This novel is a more powerful diatribe than *Untouchable* and *Coolie*. It exposes the ways by which the Britishers exploited the ignorant labourers. The trains to Assam serve as traps to transport the innocent coolies. This novel highlights the problems that the humble face in the society. The poor though virtuous are unable to out do the social oppression and suppression. Their life is a tale of continuous suffering and struggle with no end in sight. The author lays emphasis on the human dignity and humanity. His uniqueness lies in his contribution to literature in his choice of the meek as the protagonist of his fictions.

REFERENCES

Anand, Mulk Raj. *Two Leaves and a Bud* (1927).

Harrex. *The Fire and the Offering*: The English Language Novel of India 1935-70 (Calcutta: Writers Workshop, 1977) 144.

K.R.S. Iyengar. *Indian Writing in English* (New Delhi: Sterling Pub. Pvt. Ltd., 1994).

12

Mulk Raj Anand s *Coolie*: A Socio-Literary Perspective, Past and Present

EVANGELINE MANICKAM

Mulk Raj Anand s *Coolie*, a novel of deep social anger against the plight of the poor in India was published in 1936. In her Introduction to the 1985 Indian Reprint Saros Cowasjee observed that India s predicament after twenty-five years of freedom was a vindication of Anand s painful assertion of the meaninglessness of political freedom without change of heart (7). Fifty-seven years into Independence, we must with considerable shame admit that very little has changed in the lives of the poor in India, and *Coolie*, a novel of yesteryears written during the British Raj, could well be a socio-literary representation of India s struggling millions today.

Coolie, an international best seller, is Anand s most popular novel next to *Untouchable*. While the latter gave form and life to the evils of caste discrimination in society, the former details the rigours of child labour, the exploitation, cruelty and abuse of children that has taken stubborn root in the socio-economic soil of our land. The novel highlights the loss of precious childhood, the hardships and privations experienced at the hands of adults motivated by greed for gain, selfishness, heartlessness, and callousness in destroying irrevocably that tender shoot of humanity that ought to find protection and nurture from the adult world.

The story of Munoo finds all too familiar replays in the present. Drought, debt and bad harvests have led to deprivation of the family s five acres. He has watched his father die a slow death and his widowed mother succumb to her struggle against grinding poverty. At fourteen, he is farmed out of his village in the hills, to work for a family in the town losing his friends, playmates and dreams of betterment through education, to embark on a drudging routine of household chores and errands accompanied by generous insults and heaped humiliations.

While Child Labour laws exist, and the Indian Constitution bars the employment of children below the age of fourteen, it is well-known that the daily plight of millions of children is no different today than that of Anand s Munoo in 1936. NGO, World Vision of India s fundraiser pamphlet depicting the faces of needy children against the backdrop of the national flag appeals: They too need their Independence, and describes the life of Mini that closely parallels that of Munoo, only younger: eight years old, orphaned, working as a domestic servant, beaten, never paid a real life character who lives out the life of Anand s fictional Munoo. So, while many films today assert that their characters are purely fictitious and do not bear resemblance to real persons living or dead, Anand s protagonist Munoo could be any one of millions of India s children trapped early in an unending and vicious cycle of bondage and debt, finding release only in premature death.

Thus arises the question of the relevance of literature to life and to society. Social writers like Mulk Raj Anand, who finds kinship with Charles Dickens, are expected to effect social change. In their hands, literature is propagandist and meant to stir society s conscience against the terrible hurts and pain they depict. Anand s *Untouchable* (1935) won acclaim in India and abroad for its treatment of the caste problem. Yet caste is still a burning issue in India today. Likewise, *Coolie* is clearly anti-child labour in its stance, yet child labour is rampant and appears to be well on its way into twenty-first century Indian society. Literature or legislation? Which will it be to ultimately change society? Can we depend on literature to awaken social conscience and the voluntary forsaking of undesirable attitudes and practices in society; or does it take legislation to enforce the change? Then again, when legislation fails, is it the artist who must appeal to the emotions for a change of heart?

If the success of the social novel is judged by its effectiveness in achieving social change, Mulk Raj Anand s two best novels *Untouchable* and *Coolie* must be considered failures. As tools of societal change they have accomplished little. To what then does Anand s work owe its reputation and worldwide acclaim having been translated into thirty-eight languages and attracted prestigious awards? Does the story of the child Munoo create a sentimental picture of Indian life, with exotic and maudlin imagery that appeals to Western readers distanced by variance of culture? Is the recognition merely one that is awarded to an Indian writer for his excellent style and usage of the language of the British masters? One must not fail to consider the complex vocation of the artist in seeking to resolve these questions.

Does the artist work solely with a purpose towards a social cause, or does his work display a personality that is especially endowed with heightened sensibilities sensitivity to his surroundings, to the social milieu, to other human beings, so that he feels their pain, speaks their heartaches and becomes a voice of the voiceless? How do Anand s novels rate as works of Art? How does *Coolie* rate as a work of art? Is it valuable as an artistic masterpiece? Does it speak to us as a great painting speaks to us?

Even a single reading of *Coolie* gives the reader new eyes to see and opens up a whole new world. One cannot look at a rag picker, a rickshaw puller, or a domestic child servant, in the same way again. The writer suffers with his protagonist. In Anand we glimpse the writer as conscience, as he marches to a different drummer. He is not as others, ordinary, accepting. He does not see superficially but ahead of his time. Writing at a time when the underdog was not a persona for celebration or even representation, Anand looked upon the poor, the downtrodden, the outcaste with rare eyes of compassion. In a society that not only accepted but, in fact, thrived on inequality and injustice, Anand saw people as people and recognized the human soul in the lowliest individual. The inevitability of servitude in Pre-Independence India was a given. Nobody, neither the British, nor better placed Indians, could conceive of a social fabric bereft of servants, bonded labourers, slaves [ ] if truth be told. That daily life would grind to a halt without their services did not merit them just wages. Religious sanction backed caste-based inequities and the colonial set up did not require moral questioning of attitudes and treatment toward the servitor. Into such a society, Mulk Raj Anand focuses the searchlight of his perception, bringing into perspective the possibility of a renewed vision of the poor, the helpless and hopeless. His work follows in the tradition of pro-Black writers awakening the conscience of white America, smug in the complacency of the slave run economy of the South, where the Black was not recognized as human. The question of morality, Christian or otherwise, did not therefore operate with regard to their treatment. Mulk Raj Anand as a literary does artist this for India, inspiring a rethink of social values and attitudes toward the poor and needy, when no thought of the problems of the poor was considered necessary.

S.J. Patel in a study of agricultural labourers in modern India and Pakistan traces the evolution of landless labour in British India. He provides the social background and valuable insights into the period of Anand s *Coolie* which help us better appreciate Anand s achievement as a social writer and also to empathize more fully with his fictional characters. Patel asserts that Pre-British India was a self-sufficient, inter-Independent agrarian society in which landless labourers, as a class did not exist. Census returns for the first four decades of the twentieth century, however, reflect drastic changes in Indian rural society in the late nineteenth and early twentieth century. Census returns for 1931, prior to the period of publication of *Coolie* show that by then agricultural labourers came to form close to two-fifths of the agricultural population of India; their proportion virtually tripled from nearly thirteen per cent in the late nineteenth century to thirty-eight per cent in 1931, thus indicating that they had become numerically the largest group, a remarkable increase that reflects the most dramatic social transformation in the entire history of Indian rural society (49).

This disintegration of the traditional agrarian society and the increase in the size of the newly born class of landless agricultural labourers is attributed to the land policies pursued by the British in India from late eighteenth century onward.

The British introduced the zamindari settlement, which created large individual landlords in the eastern region in 1793; the raiyatwari settlement, which dealt with individual small peasant landlords in the Southern Triangle; and the mahalwari settlement, which dealt with the village elders in their capacity as landlords in the North. They completely sidetracked the traditional institution of village community in all these settlements and overhauled the manner and mode of revenue payment. The Act of 1793 declared former tax-gathers (zamindars) who were no more than agents of the former governments for the collection of land revenue, full proprietors of the area over which their rights of revenue collection extended. Thus, millions of landholders and cultivators were rudely dispossessed and turned overnight from proprietors to tenants at will. Patel attributes this to British greed: In the whole history of mankind, ancient or modern, one would look in vain for a parallel to this classic example wherein so many were sacrificed in such a short time so that a few may prosper or rule (55).

In the raiyatwari system, the individual cultivator was expected to pay a fixed sum of cash to the government twice a year crop or no crop. Failure to pay the revenue in time resulted in forfeiture of land. Cultivators had never handled coin in their lives since circulation of money in the countryside had barely developed, and were poor in pecuniary terms, unable to convert superfluity of grain into money for taxes. Land hitherto unsaleable in Pre-British India, and valueless until cultivated, was made transferable by law under the British, with legal machinery to enforce the transfers. Land thus became a security against monetary advances and eligible for foreclosure. As cultivators sank deeper into debt during years of famine, sickness and natural calamities, their property easily passed out of their hands. Thus the dispossession of the peasantry swelled the ranks of landless labour in British India.

Indistinguishable in status from the landless labourers, but not categorized as such, were the large group of dwarf-holding labourers. These were petty cultivators who held less than five acres of land but were in fact no better off than their landless counterparts. They were exploited by middlemen and absentee landlords who gained a greater margin of profit by sharecropping their land rather than through employment of landless labour. On an average, more than half the farmers in the country cultivated small patches of less than five acres as dwarf-holders, maintaining a very precarious hold on their land and, being prey to circumstances, were likely to lose it at anytime.

Given this background, it is not difficult to contextualize the life story of Anand s Munoo who, at the opening of the novel, recalls the circumstances in which his father is divested of his five acres by the landlord to whom he owed rent money and interest on his mortgage. The loss of the land leads the family to rack and ruin and catapults the orphaned boy into his own interminable struggle as a child labourer.

Coolie has a very simple linear plot structure. The action begins when fourteen-year-old orphan, Munoo, has to leave his village home to earn his livelihood in the town. The novel follows a picaresque tradition as Munoo goes from misadventure to misadventure to untimely death. First, he is placed as a domestic servant with a family in the town of Sham Nagar. This turns out to be a painful experience. He runs away and is taken by Seth Prabha Dyal whom he meets on the train, to his home at Daulatpur, where he earns his keep working in his benefactor s jam and pickle enterprise. When the business fails and his master goes bankrupt, Munoo is left to fend for himself as a coolie in the vegetable market and the railway station. Next, he moves to Bombay, where he joins the great masses struggling to eke out a living in the great city. Finally, an accident brings him back to the hills, to Simla, where he works for an Anglo-Indian lady, as her rickshaw puller. Munoo is only sixteen when he dies of tuberculosis. In his death Anand evokes a reader response similar to Dickens evocation, at the death of little Nell in *The Old Curiosity Shop*. It is a sadness that comes at the prolonged suffering and needless death of the young and the innocent.

In Munoo, Anand describes a boy who is reluctant to leave home, giving up his childhood, pleasant days of companionship, and his education: For in spite of the fact that his aunt was always abusing him, in spite of the fact that she ordered him about [ ] in spite of the fact that she beat him more than he beat his cattle, he really did not want to go to the town. At least not yet (19).

He has no inkling of what lies ahead and is surprised to see hill folk like himself in the town as they carried weights on their backs [...]. He could not realize the significance of this world (19). His initial awe at the novelty of town life gives way to despair as he is unaccustomed to housework, is nagged and harassed by the woman of the house, and experiences first-hand the divide between servant and employer, between rich and poor. He is not allowed play with the children of the family, to gawk at visitors, or to indulge his childhood curiosity to watch with fascination the gramophone being played. He embarrasses himself and earns the curses of his employers on the very first day when he relieves himself against the steps of their home.

What does Child Labour do to the heart of a child? Munoo s soul is slowly crushed. The happy child, curious wonderstruck, tracing the colours, the shapes and sizes of all things, enquiring into their meanings (44) yearns for love, is stung by insults and slowly settles into the routine of domestic slavery, though not easily: the wild bird of his heart fluttered every now and then with the desire for happiness. His identity is clarified for him: It did not occur to him to ask himself what he was apart from being a servant. He promises himself that he would be a good servant, a perfect model of a servant, and soon learns to accept a lower status: These people were superior [ ]. What constituted their superiority, he did not know [ ] thoroughly convinced of his inferiority, he accepted his position as a slave and tried to instill into his mind the notion of his brutishness that his mistress had so often nagged him about (44-48).

Coolie highlights the causes and effects of migration through the predicament of Munoo. Poverty forces people from the villages to migrate to the towns and cities in search of a livelihood as Munoo is forced to Sham Nagar, then to Daulatabad and on to Bombay. Whether children take up employment to augment family income or to support themselves, adults exploit them and appropriate their earnings. Most often there is a relative collecting on their behalf: How can I get you the clothes you want, and shoes, if you spend all the pay money which I am keeping for you? says his uncle Daya Ram, when Munoo ask for some money for food (61). They are never paid: We need another boy to run errands and do odd jobs. And it seems, he will be glad enough to have the food, and we need not pay him, speculates Prabha s partner when he suggests taking the runaway Munoo home with them from the train (79).

Whatever the apprehensions and sadness at leaving home, migration provides hope hope of freedom from starvation, and the prospect of a better life. As the train nears Daulatabad city Munoo experiences a curious flutter of excitement in his heart, like the thrill of fear and happiness which had filled him when he first laid eyes on Sham Nagar the fear of the unknown in his bowels and the stirring of hope for a wonderful life in the new world he was entering (81). It is the same excitement that calms his overwhelming fears on approaching Bombay, as his heart lightened for a moment with the joy of seeing the sea for the first time in his life (175). But disillusionment is inevitable: The bigger the city, the more cruel it is to the sons of Adam (177). Wherever he goes there is pain and struggle and hopelessness. In Sham Nagar, it did not take long for him to wake up to the rude reality of his true status and the menial life he was fated to in Babu Nathu Ram s household. In Bombay his heart sank: Even here the coolies sleep in the street! He suddenly realised, and the memory of the words of the coolie who had said money was strewn about the streets of Bombay sounded falsely hollow in his brain (179).

The importance of money emphasized again and again in the novel must be seen against the background of bonded labour in the agrarian set up of the 1930s. The immediate cause of slavery and bondage in India was monetary. The relationship of debtor and creditor in rural India evolved into virtual slavery for the former and absolute dominance by the latter because of the need for advances of money, and the inability to repay. Systems of guaranteed subsistence broke down with the disintegration of the traditional systems, and menials had to accept bondage to avoid starvation. Absence of means to livelihood meant the bondmen were freed only to starve. The prevalent situation ensured that nearly half of farm servants were monetary bonded labourers a system that Patel notes could not have existed in the non-monetary economy of the earlier century (63).

> Money is everything, his uncle had said on the day of his journey to town. Money is, indeed everything, Munoo thought. And his mind dwelt for the first time on the difference between himself, the poor boy, and his masters, the rich people, between all the poor people in his village and [ ] the landlord.
>
> But there were so many people, so many poor people and only one or two rich people in his village [ ]. In the town, of course, there seemed many more rich people than poor people. But then he had been told in school, there were hundreds of villages for one town, and if there were as many poor people in all the villages as there were in his, surely there were many more poor people in the world than rich [ ].
>
> Whether there were more rich or more poor people, there seemed to be only two kinds of people in the world. Caste did not matter. I am a Kshatriya and I am poor [ ]. No, caste does not matter [ ] all servants look alike: there must be only two kinds of people in the world: the rich and the poor. (69)

In Bombay, again, the protestors recognized,

> There are only two kinds of people in the world, the rich and the poor [ ] and between the two there is no connection. The rich and the powerful, [ ] whose opulence is built on robbery and theft [ ] are honoured and admired by the whole world [ ] you the poor and the humble [ ] swindled out of your rights and broken in body and soul are respected by no one. (266-67)

Munoo s life comes full circle when he leaves Bombay and is brought to Simla. Again, it is to someone else s convenience: Mrs Mainwaring, like Prabha before him, sees in him a potentially good servant. The description of his illness and death by tuberculosis is oppressive. It is understandable only in the sociological and historical context: This was the fate of many like him at the time. Bringing the story up into the present that seems justified considering legislation and time have brought little change we think of Munoo s dreams for his future, as a young student in fifth class, an aspiring engineer: He had dreamed, of course, of all the wonderful things which the village folk spoke about when they came back from the towns [ ]. He was especially interested in machines such as he had read about in the science premier of the fourth class. But he had meant to go to town when he had passed all his examination here and was ready to learn to make machines himself (11-12).

Viewed from a modern vantage point also, Munoo represents the typical victim of circumstances that push children into the work force. Helen Sekar and Noor Mohammed in their study *Child Labour in Home Based Lock Industries of Aligarh,* make pertinent observations regarding child labour in a specific context, but which apply in general as well:

> Child labour is rampant in small manufacturing units, which employ labour intensive techniques. (35)
>
> Extreme poverty is the cause of child labour. Working children migrate to the city due to poverty. Migrant households seek hope of a better employment. (57)
>
> Child labourers are individual workers on a time-rate basis working five to ten hours daily. They are very low paid, have no social security and are unorganized. (131)
>
> 80% of child workers suffering chronic illness have occupational diseases, TB, Asthma, Cardiac problems, mental problems. (132)
>
> A majority of children are positive about education. They like to go to school, but are pulled out by their parents due to financial hardship for earning. The drop out rate is highest in the fourth and fifth standard. (138)
>
> Sekar and Mohammed perceive no major change in the wake of legislation. Implementation of Labour Legislation is ineffective. (120)

What hope then do we have to offer the Munoos of today? President Abdul Kalam in *INDIA 2020: A Vision for the New Millennium,* envisions positive change in Indian society by the year 2020. He focuses on the Agricultural sector and suggests remedies for the plight of farmers; the Health sector especially health care provision to the poor, AIDS, tuberculosis and other major challenges to public health; Child Labour; and Education. He expresses a compassionate view in the dispensing of health care: Health administrators should learn to treat health as people s pain and agony, not as files. Similarly politicians at all levels should learn to look at pain removal as a part of their duty (240). Children hold a special place in his estimation: I would not like to give any special message to young children because they themselves are born with the message. They are fresh. I would therefore appeal to parents and teachers not to pollute their fresh minds with our own frustrations. If we can instead convey to them the message about a bright future and encourage them, that will be a great service we will be doing to them and also to the country (293). It is hoped this message will take root and spread so that his vision may become a reality for the deprived children of India to realize their dreams and fulfill their potential for the future.

WORKS CITED

Anand, Mulk Raj. *Coolie.* 1936. Delhi: Arnold Heinemann, 1985. All textual references are taken from this edition.

Kalam, Abdul A.P.J. with Y.S. Rajan. *India 2020: A Vision for the New Millennium.* New Delhi: Viking, 1998.

Patel, S.J. Agricultural Labourers in Modern India and Pakistan. *Indian Journal of Economics,* vol. XXXIII, July, 1952. *The World of the Rural Labourer in Colonial India.* Ed. Gyan Prakash, Delhi: OUP, 1992: 47-75.

Sekar, Helen R. and Noor Mohammed. *Child Labour in Home Based Lock Industries of Aligarh.* Noida: V.V. Giri National Labour Institute, 2001.

Bibliography

A. PRIMARY SOURCES

I. Novels

Untouchable (with an introduction by E.M. Forster). London: Laurence and Wishart, 1935. London: Bodley Head, 1970. Toronto: Copp Clark, 1970. Harmondsworth. Penguin Books, 1986. Bombay: Kutub-Popular, 1950. Delhi, Hind Pocket Books, 1970.

Coolie. London: Laurence and Wishart, 1936. New York: Liberty Press, 1952. Bombay: Current Book House, 1953. London: The Bodley Head, 1972. Toronto: Copp Clark, 1972. Delhi: Hind Pocket Books, 1973. New Delhi: My Fair Paperbacks, 1981. New Delhi: Penguin Books, 1993.

Two Leaves and a Bud. London: Laurence and Wishart, 1937. Bombay: Kutub-Popular, 1946. New York: Liberty Press, 1954. Delhi: Orient Paperbacks, n.d. New Delhi: My Fair Paperbacks, 1981.

Lament on the Death of a Master of Arts. Lucknow: Naya Sansar, 1938. Delhi: Hind Pocket Books, 1967.

The Village. London: Jonathan Cape, 1939. Bombay: Kutub-Popular, 1960. Delhi: Orient Paperbacks, n.d.

Across the Black Waters. London: Jonathan Cape, 1940. Bombay: Kutub-Popular, 1955. Delhi: Vision Books, 1940. New Delhi: Orient Paperbacks, 1980.

The Sword and the Sickle. London: Jonathan Cape, 1942. Bombay: Kutub-Popular, 1955. New Delhi: Arnold Heinemann, 1984.

The Big Heart. London: Hutchinson, 1945. Madras: Subbaiah Chetty, 1947. Bombay: Kutub-Popular, n.d. New Delhi: Arnold Heinemann, 1980.

Seven Summers: *The Story of an Indian Childhood.* London: Hutchinson, 1951. Bombay: Kutub-Popular, 1960. New Delhi: Orient Paperbacks, 1970. Arnold Heinemann, 1986.

Private Life of an Indian Prince. London: Hutchinson, 1953. Toronto: Copp Clark, 1970. Delhi: Hind Pocket Books, 1972.

The Old Woman and the Cow. Bombay: Kutub-Popular, 1960. republished as *Gauri.* Delhi: Arnold Heinemann, 1960, 1981. Delhi: Hind Pocket Books, 1976.

The Road. Bombay: Kutub-Popular, 1961. New Delhi, Sterling Publishers, 1974, 1987.

Death of a Hero: Epitaph for Maqbool Sherwan. Bombay: Kutub-Popular, 1963. Delhi: Orient Paperbacks, n.d. New Delhi: Arnold Heinemann, 1985.

Morning Face. Bombay: Kutub-Popular, 1968. Delhi: Arnold Heinemann, 1976.

Confession of a Lover. New Delhi: Arnold Heinemann, 1976.

The Bubble. New Delhi: Arnold Heinemann, 1984.

Little Plays of Mahatma Gandhi (a novel in dramatic dialogues). New Delhi: Arnold Hienemann, 1992.

Nine Moods of Bharata. New Delhi: Arnold Associates, 1998.

II. Short Story Collections

The Lost Child and Other Stories. London: J.A. Allen, 1934.

The Barber's Trade Union and Other Stories. London: Jonathan Cape, 1944. New Delhi: Arnold Heinemann, 1944. Delhi: Orient May Fair Paperbacks, 1977.

The Tractor and the Corn Goddess and Other Stories. Bombay: Thacker and Company, 1947.

Reflection on the Golden Bed and other Stories. Bombay: Current Book House, 1954. New Delhi: Arnold Publishers, 1989.

Selected Stories. Moscow: Foreign Languages Publishing House, 1954, 1955.

The Power of Darkness and Other Stories. Bombay: Jaico Publishers, 1959.

Lajwanti and Other Stories. Bombay: Jaico Publishers, 1966.

Between Tears and Laughter. New Delhi: Sterling Publishers, 1973, 1991.

Folk Tales of Punjab. New Delhi: Sterling Publishers, 1974.

Selected Short Stories. ed. M.K. Naik. New Delhi: Arnold Heinemann, 1977.

The Lost Child and Two Lyrical Stories. New Delhi: Abhinav Publications, 1995.

Anand, Mulk Raj and Iqbal Singh, eds. *Indian Short Stories.* London: The New Indian Publishing House, 1946.

Anand, Mulk Raj and S. Babu Rao. *Panorama: An Anthology of Modern Indian Short Stories.* New Delhi: Sterling Publishers, 1986.

For Children

Indian Fairy Tales (Retold). Bombay: Kutub-Popular, 1946. Rpt. 1966.

The Story of Man. Amritsar: Sikh Publishing House, 1952.

The Story of the Indian Post Offices. New Delhi: Post and Telegraph Department, 1954.

More Indian Fairy Tales (Retold). Bombay: Kutub-Popular, 1958.

Aesop□s Fables (Retold). Bombay: Dhawante-Popular, 1960.

The Story of Chacha Nehru. Bombay: Rajpal & Sons, 1965.

A Day in the Life of Mohenjo-Daro. New Delhi: Children s Book Trust, 1968.

III. Non-Fiction

(Select articles and books mostly related to critical and creative writings)

Toward a New Indian Literature. *Left Review* 2.12 (1936).

Letter to the Editor on *Two Leaves and a Bud. Spectator* 5685 (1937).

Letter to the Editor on *Two Leaves and a Bud. Spectator* 5697 (1937).

English Novels of the Twentieth Century on India. *Asiatic Review* 39.139 (1943).

I Believe in Man. *In Search of Faith.* ed. Ernest W. Martin. London: Lindsay Drummond, 1943.

Where is the English Novel? *Our Time* 3.6 (1943).

Novelists in Exile. *Our Time* 4 (1945).

Apology of Heroism. Bombay: Kutub-Popular, 1946. Delhi: May Fair Paperbacks, 1975.

Introduction to *Rice and Other Stories* by K.A. Abbas. Bombay: Kutub-Popular, 1947.

The King Emperor□s English. Bombay: Hind Kitabs, 1948.

A Writer s Confession of His Faith. *Bharat Jyoti,* 27 Apr. 1952.

The Continuity of Tradition. *Marg* 9.1 (1955).

The Emergence of the Hero in the Modern Indian Novel. *Illustrated Weekly of India* 9 Dec. 1956: 42-49.

Trends in the Novel. *Cultural Forum* Nov. 1961. Tagore Number.

New Bearing in Indian Literature. *Literary Review* 4.4 (1961). Anand was the guest editor of this issue.

Is Indian Literature Sufficiently Indian ? *United Asia* 13.6 (1961).

The Writer at Bay. *Seminar* May, 1961.

International Literary Seminar. *Cultural Forum* 4.3 (1962).

The Writer s Role in National Integration: A Discussion. *Indian Literature* 5.1 (1962).

Creative Writing in the Present Crisis. *Indian Literature* 6.1 (1963).

The Concept of an Asian Mind. *Contemporary Indian Literature* 4 (1964).

Shaw Talks to Shakespeare. *Cultural Forum* 6.3 (1964).

Letter to E.M. Forster. *E.M. Forster: A Tribute.* ed. K. Natwar Singh. New York: Harcourt, Brace & World, 1964.

East-West Dialogue. *Indian Writers in Conference.* Ed. Nissim Ezekiel. Bombay: P.E.N. All India Centre, 1964.

What Shakespeare Means to Me ? *Contemporary Indian Literature* 5, 6-7 (1965).

How I Became a Writer ? *Contemporary Indian Literature* 5.11-12 (1965). Rpt. in *Mirror* May 1977.

A Note on Modern Indian Fiction. *Indian Literature* 8.1 (1965). 44-57.

Is Universal Criticism Possible ? *Literary Criterion* 7.1 (1965): 68-75. Rpt. in *Literary Criticism: European and Indian Traditions.* Ed. C.D. Narasimhaiah. Mysore: University of Mysore Press, 1966.

The Role of Creative Writers and Artists in the Developing Countries of Afro-Asia. *Afro-Asia and World Affairs* 3.1 (1966): 18-21.

Modernism in Indian and Soviet Literature. *Amity* 4.1 (1966): 44-47.

The Krishna Theme in Indian Art: The Best of Lovers. *Cultural Forum* 9.1-2 (1967-1968).

The Sources of Creative Writing. *Indian Literature* 7 (Sep. 1967).

The Story of My Experiment with a White Lie. *Indian Literature* 10.3 (July-Sep., 1967): 28-43. Rpt. in Naik, et al. *Critical Essays.* Madras: Macmillan, 1979. 4-18.

At What Price, My Brother. *Indian Literature* 1.1 (1967): 52-60.

Folk Tradition as an Aid to Modern Expression. *Indo-Asian Culture* 17.3 (1968): 3-6.

The Task Before the Writer. *Indian Culture* 6.1 (1963): 70-77.

The Question of Modernity. *Modernity and Contemporary Indian Literature.* Simla: Indian Institute of Advanced Study, 1968.

Writer s Role in Modern Society. *Contemporary Indian Literature* 9.1 (Jan. 1969).

Profile of E.M. Forster. *Literary Half-Yearly* 10.2 (1969).

Old Myths and New Myths Recital *versus* Novel. *Banasthali Patrika* 5.13 (1969): 27-36. Rpt. in Narasimhaiah, *Indian Literature of the Past Fifty Years.* Mysore: University of Mysore Publication, 1970. 109-20.

What Good is Literature For? *Banasthali Patrika* 5.14 (1970): 81-83.

About the Lost Child and Other Allegories. *Indian Literature* 13.1 (1970): 28.

Pigeon-Indian: Some Notes on Indian English Writing. *Studies in Australian and Indian Literature.* Eds. Narasimhaiah and Nagarajan. New Delhi: Indian Council of Cultural Relations, 1971, 228-48. *Journal of Karnatak University* (Humanities), 1972: 69-90. Also in *World Literature Written in English* 21.2 (1982): 325-36.

The Changling An Indo-Anglian Novelist s Credo. *Indian and Foreign Review* 9.23 (1972).

Roots and Flowers: Two Lectures on the Metamorphosis of Technique and Content in the Indian Novel. Dharwad: Karnatak University Press, 1972.

Author to Critic: The Letters of Mulk Raj Anand to Saros Cowasjee. Ed. Saros Cowasjee, Calcutta: Writers Workshop, 1973.

Trends in the Modern Indian Novel. *Journal of Indian Writing in English* 1.1 (1973): 1-6.

The Rhythms of Indian Life On Indian English. *Research and Criticism.* Ed. Radhakrishnan. Annamalai: Research Scholar Association 1975. 59-61.

The Changling. *World Literature Written in English.* 15.1(1976): 110-20. Also in *Journal of English Studies* (Warangal) 4.1 (1972): 229-38.

The Humanism of M.K. Gandhi. Bombay: Tata Press, n.d.

On the Use of Epithets, Swear Words, Curses and Imprecations. *Littcrit* 3, 2.2 (1976): 1-5.

Literature s Revolutionary Message. *Youth Times* Oct. 28, Nov. 10, 1977.

The Meaning of Words. *Mirror* Sep. 1977.

An Undeclared War (The Internecine war between Brown Sahibs and Babus). *Littcrit* 4, 3.1 (1978): 11-24.

Why I Write? *Indo-English Literature.* Ed. K.K. Sharma. Ghaziabad: Vimal Prakashan, 1977. 9-22. Rpt. in *Kakatiya Journal of English Studies* 2.1 (1977): 244-55. Also in Sharma, K.K. *Perspectives on Mulk Raj Anand.* Ghaziabad: Vimal Prakashan, 1978. 1-6.

Creative Process. *Littcrit* 6, 4.1 (1978): 1-3.

My Childhood. *Indian Literary Review* 1.1 (1978): 37-40.

The Continuity of Myths, Symbols and Images. *Marg* 32.1 (1978): 5-8.

Pigeon-Irish and Pigeon-Indian. *Commonwealth Quarterly* 3.10 (1979).

Reflections of a Novelist. *Tribune* 5 May 1979.

Reflections of a Novelist: Some Notes on the Novel. *Journal of Literature and Aesthetics* 2.2-3 (1982): 132-36.

Images and Words. *Illustrated Weekly of India* 8 June 1980.

Old Myth and New Myth. *Marg* 33.4 (1980): 40A.

Narcissism or Solidarity. *Osmania Journal of English Studies* 1983: 19-26.

Conversations in Bloomsbury. New Delhi: Arnold Heinemann, 1981.

The First and Last Impact of E.M. Forster: Some Reminiscences. *Approaches to E.M. Forster: A Centenary Volume.* Ed. V.A. Shahane, New Delhi: Arnold Heinemann, 1981.

Content and Form in *Untouchable* and *Kanthapura.*□ *Littcrit* 14, 8.1 (1982): 47-60.

As I Walk Along Gorky Street. *Tribune* 22 Nov. 1987.

Compulsion for Creativity. *Tribune* 8 May 1988.

Intellectual Statesman. *Tribune* 3 Jan. 1988.

Destination Man: Nehru s Vision of New Order. *Tribune* 12 Nov. 1989.

The Sources of Protest in My Novels. *Literary Criterion* 18.4 (1983): 1-12.

Afterword. *Response: Recent Revelations.* Ed. Hari Mohan Prasad. Bareilly: Prakash Book Depot, 1983. 307-35.

The Relevance of Indian-English Literature. *Criticism and Research* 7 (1984-85): 172-80.

English is a valid Literary Medium. *Times of India* 26 May 1990: 8.

Many Obstacles to Free Media. *Times of India* 10 Jan. 1990: 7.1-6.

Is Indian English Literature *Deshi* or *Videshi?*□ *Indian Book Chronicle* June 1990: 15-16.

Pigeon-Indian: A Note on the Emergence of Indian English Literature. *Journal of Indian Writing in English* 20.1-2 (1992): 1-3.

R. Tagore: The founder of the Indian Novel. *Viswabharati Quarterly* 2.1-4 (1991-1992).

Rhythm Is What Is Common to All Heightened Expression. *Literary Criterion* 28.4 (1993): 81-87.

Mulk Raj Anand Remembers. *Indian Literature* 36.2 (1993) 176-86.

Old Myth and New Myth: Letters from Mulk Raj Anand to K.V.S. Murti. Calcutta: Writers Workshop, 1992.

IV. Interviews

Bald, Suresh Renjen. Interview (personal). 24 July 1971.

Chatterjee. A Very Personal View. *Youth Times* 5 Apr. 1974: 22.

Eskay. Interview with Mulk Raj Anand. *Patriot* 28 May 1982: 2.

Fisher, Marlene. A Day with Mulk Raj Anand. *Illustrated Weekly of India* 12 Aug. 1973: 44-45.

. Interview with Mulk Raj Anand. *World Literature Written in English* 13.1P (1974): 109-22.

Jafri, Sultana. Mulk Raj Anand: Remove the Threat of War. Interview. *Soviet Land* Dec. 1985: 30.

Khandala. Conversation with Mulk Raj Anand (Tape), 19 May 1973.

Lalji, Mishra. Interview with Mulk Raj Anand. *Creative Forum* 2-2-1989.

Mathur, O.P. Anand on Society and Literature. Excerpts from an Interview with Mulk Raj Anand. *Mulk Raj Anand: A Home Appraisal.* Ed. Atma Ram. Hoshiarpur: Charravak Publications, 1988. 162-76. Rpt. in Mathur, *Modern Indian English Fiction.* Delhi: Abhinav Publications, 1993. 192-02.

Nahal, Chaman. Speak up for the Down and Out. Interview with Mulk Raj Anand. *Hindustan Times* 24 Dec. 1995: 13.

Rajan, P.K. A Decadent Society Needs Renewal. *Hindu* 11 Dec. 1983: 22.

. A Dialogue with Mulk Raj Anand. Rajan, *Studies in Mulk Raj Anand.* Delhi Abhinav Publications, 1986.

Ram, Atma. Interview with Mulk Raj Anand. Ram, *Interviews With Indian English Writers.* Calcutta: Writers Workshop, 1983. 9-20.

Ratan, Jai. Meeting with Mulk Raj Anand. *Miscellany* 8, Sep.-Oct. 1961.

Sahgal, Pavan. Experiment with an Alien Tongue. Interview. *Times Weekly* 13 May 1973, 15.

Samatharaj, Dipak. A Conversation with Mulk Raj Anand. *Chandrabhaga* 9 & 10 (1983): 113-23.

Sethi, Vijaya Mohan. Short Stories of Mulk Raj Anand. Interview. *Punjab Journal of English Studies* 3 (1988): 73-80. Also in Sethi *Mulk Raj Anand. The Short Story Writer.* New Delhi: Ashish Publishing House, 1990. 17-27.

Singh, Sushila. The Lost Child at 80s. Interview with Mulk Raj Anand. *Times of India* 8 Dec. 1985.

Verma, K.D. An Interview with Mulk Raj Anand. *South Asian Review* 15.12 (July, 1991): 31-38.

B. SECONDARY SOURCES: CRITICAL WORKS

I. Bibliographies

Bibliography of the Novels and Stories by Mulk Raj Anand in various languages. *Contemporary Indian Literature* V. 1965.

Cowasjee, Saros. Select Bibliography. *So Many Freedoms.* Delhi: Oxford University Press, 1977. 191-200.

Packham, G. *Mulk Raj Anand: A Checklist.* Mysore: Literary Press, 1978.

Paul, Premila. Bibliography. *The Novels of Mulk Raj Anand. A Thematic Study.* New Delhi: Sterling Publishers, 1983. 164-80.

Ram, Atma, ed. Select Bibliography. *Mulk Raj Anand: A Home Appraisal.* Hoshiarpur: Chaarvak Publications, 1988: 231-53.

Seth, Vijayanand. Select Bibliography. *Mulk Raj Anand: The Short Story Writer.* New Delhi: Ashish Publishing House, 1990. 92-97.

Sharma, K.K. Comp. Select Bibliography. *Perspectives on Mulk Raj Anand.* Ghaziabad (Delhi): Vimal Prakashan, 1978: 181-86.

II. Special Issues

Contemporary Indian Literature 5.11-12 (1965). Special Issue on Mulk Raj Anand. Nov.-Dec. 1965.

Kakatiya Journal of English Studies 2.1 (1977). Special Number on Mulk Raj Anand.

III. Books

Abidi, S.Z.H. *Mulk Raj Anand's Untouchable: A Critical Study.* Bareilly: Prakash Book Depot, 1972.

. *Mulk Raj Anand's Coolie: A Critical Study.* Bareilly: Prakash Book Depot, 1976.

Agnihotri, G.N. *Indian Life and Problems in the Novels of Mulk Raj Anand, Raja Rao and R.K. Narayan.* Meerut: Shalabh Book House, 1984.

Anjaneyulu, T. *Critical Study of the Selected Novels of Mulk Raj Anand, Manohar Malgonkar and Khushwant Singh.* New Delhi: Atlantic Publishers, 1997.

Berry, Margaret. *Mulk Raj Anand: The Man and the Novelist.* Amsterdam: Oriental Press, 1971.

Cowasjee, Saros. *Author to Critic: The Letters of M.R. Anand to Saros Cowasjee.* Calcutta: Writers Workshop, 1973.

. *Coolie: An Assessment.* New Delhi: Oxford University Press, 1976.

. *So Many Freedoms.* New Delhi: Oxford University Press, 1977.

Dhar, T.N. *History-Fiction Interface: M.R. Anand, Nayantara Sahgal, Salman Rushdie, Shashi Taroor and O.V. Vijayan.* New Delhi: Prestige Books, 1999.

Dhawan, R.K., ed. *The Novels of Mulk Raj Anand.* New Delhi: Prestige Books, 1992.

Fisher, Marlene. *The Wisdom of the Heart: A Study of the Works of Mulk Raj Anand.* New Delhi: Sterling Publishers, 1985.

Gautam, G.L. *Mulk Raj Anand's Critique of Religious Fundamentalism: A Critical Assessment of His Novels.* Delhi: Kanti Publishers, 1996.

George, C.J. *Mulk Raj Anand: His Art and His Concerns.* New Delhi: Atlantic Publishers, 1994.

Gupta, G.S. Balarama. *Mulk Raj Anand: A Study of His Fiction in Human Perspective.* Bareilly: Prakash Book Depot, 1974.

Khan, S.A. *The Novel of Commitment: Mulk Raj Anand.* New Delhi: Atlantic Publishers, 1999.

Lindsay, Jack. *The Elephant and the Lotus.* Bombay: Kutub-Populars, 1965.

. *Mulk Raj Anand: A Critical Essay.* Bombay: Hind Kitabs, 1948.

Murti, K.V.S. *The Sword and the Sickle: A Study of Mulk Raj Anand's Novels.* Mysore: Geetha Book House Publishers, 1983.

. *Old Myth and New Myth: Letters from Mulk Raj Anand to K.V.S. Murti.* Calcutta: Writers Workshop, 1992.

Naik, M.K. *Mulk Raj Anand.* New Delhi: Arnold Heinemann, 1973.

Nasini, Reza Ahmed. *Language of Mulk Raj Anand, Raja Rao and R.K. Narayan.* New Delhi: Capital Publishing House, 1989.

Niven, Alastair. *The Yoke of Pity: A Study in the Fictional Writing of Mulk Raj Anand.* New Delhi: Arnold Heinemann, 1978.

Paul, Premila. *The Novels of Mulk Raj Anand: A Thematic Study.* New Delhi: Sterling Publishers, 1983.

Prasad, Shaileswar Sati. *Insulated and the Injured* (on Mulk Raj Anand). Patna: Janaki Prakashan, 1997.

Rajan, P.K. *Studies in Mulk Raj Anand.* Delhi: Abhinav Publications, 1986.

. *Mulk Raj Anand: A Revaluation.* New Delhi: Arnold Associates, 1994.

Ram, Atma, ed. *Mulk Raj Anand: A Home Appraisal.* Hoshiarpur: Chaarvak Publications, 1988.

Ramamurthy, S. *The Novels of Charles Dickens and Mulk Raj Anand.* Trichy: By the Author, 1994.

Riemenschneider, Dieter. *An Ideal Man in Mulk Raj Anand's Novels.* Bombay: Kutub-Populars, 1967.

Sethi, Vijay Mohan. *Mulk Raj Anand: The Short Story Writer.* New Delhi: Ashish Publishing House, 1990.

Sharma, K.K., ed. *Perspectives on Mulk Raj Anand.* Ghaziabad: Vimal Prakashan, 1978.

Sharma, Ambuj Kumar. *The Theme of Exploitation in the Novels of Mulk Raj Anand.* New Delhi: Deep & Deep Publications, 1990.

Singh, Vaidyanath. *Social Realism in the Fiction of Dickens and Mulk Raj Anand.* New Delhi: Commonwealth Publishers, 1997.

Sinha, K.N. *Mulk Raj Anand.* New York: Twayne Publications, 1972.

IV. Research Articles

Agnihotri, G.N. Mulk Raj Anand His Progressive Proletarianism Agnihotri 61-82.

Alcock, Peter. Some Thing Different: Problems of Cultural Relativism in Non-European Literature. *ACLALS Bulletin* 5th ser 1 (1978): 48-66.

Amur, G.S. Individual Consciousness and Social Reality in Mulk Raj Anand s *Untouchable* and Shivatam Karanth s *Choma's Drum.* Amur, *Essays* 117-29.

Anand *World Authors 1950-1970.* 50-53.

Arora, V.N. Mulk Raj Anand s Claim to Fame. *English Association Journal* (1965): 26-30.

Asnani, Shyam M. Untouchability and Mulk Raj Anand s *Untouchable.* *Banasthali Patrika* 6.16 (1971): 31-36.

. Socio-Political Concerns in the Novels of Mulk Raj Anand. *Triveni* 45.1 (1976): 38-50.

. The Theme of East-West Encounter in the Novels of Mulk Raj Anand. *Littcrit* 7, 4.2 (1978): 11-19.

. A Critique of Mulk Raj Anand s Literary Creed. *Commonwealth Quarterly* 4.15 (1988): 64-85. Rpt. in Asnani *New Dimensions* 116-31 (1988).

. Form and Technique in Mulk Raj Anand s Novels. *Indian Scholar* 2.2 (1980): 89-103.

. The Indian Princes: Their Portrayal in the Indo-English Novel. *Commonwealth Quarterly* 3.2 (1979), 85-104 Rpt. in Asnani, *Critical Response* 62-78.

. Social Protest in Mulk Raj Anand. Asnani, *Critical Response,* 10-24.

. Mulk Raj Anand and the Bloomsbury Elite Group . Ram, *Mulk Raj Anand: A Home Appraisal* 149-61.

. New Morality in the Modern Indo-English Novel, A Study of Mulk Raj Anand, Anita Desai and Nayantara Sahgal. *Language Forum* 9.1-4 (1981-82): 30-50. Rpt. in Dhawan, *The Novels of Mulk Raj Anand* 39-49.

. Mulk Raj Anand: Of Crushed Humanity. Ross 75-87.

Aston, N.M. Mulk Raj Anand s *Death of a Hero:* A Study. *Commonwealth Review* 5.2 (1993-94): 101-06. Rpt. in Dhawan, *Indian Literature Today.*

Awasthi, Kamal N. *The Sword and the Sickle:* A Study in Heroic Consciousness. Ram, *Mulk Raj Anand: A Home Appraisal* 111-26.

Bais, H.S.S. An Endless Search: A Psycho-Analytical Study of Anant in Mulk Raj Anand s *The Big Heart.* Pathak, *Indian Fiction in English* 38-46.

Bald, Suresh Renjen. Politics of a Revolutionary Elite: A Study of Mulk Raj Anand s Novels. *Modern Asian Studies* 8 (1974): 473-89.

Bande, Usha. Gauri-Myth and Reality. Ram, *Mulk Raj Anand: A Home Appraisal.* 60-75.

Banerjee, Surabhi. Irony as a Stylistic Device: A Note on the Opening Chapter of Anand s *Across the Black-Waters. Journal of Literature and Aesthetics* 2.2-3 (1982): 63-66.

Berry, Margaret. Purpose in the Novels of Mulk Raj Anand. *Mahfil* 5 (1969): 85-90.

. India: A Double Key. *Journal of Indian Writing in English* 6.1 (1978): 31-38.

Bhaskaran, Gautam. Writer as a Town Planner: Anand, M.R. *Statesman* 29 Nov. 1983: 5.

Bhatnagar, K.C. Mulk Raj Anand: Poetic Realism and Protest. Bhatnagar, K.C., *Realism* 131-69.

Bhatt, Sanjay. The Lost Child. *Kakatiya Journal of English Studies* 2.1 (1977): 219-22. Also in Dhawan, *The Novels of Mulk Raj Anand* 123-25.

Bhattacharya, B.K. *Two Leaves and a Bud:* Truth and Fiction. *Kakatiya Journal of English Studies* 2.1 (1977): 39-47.

Boparai, H. Singh. The Adamic Myth and *Two Leaves and a Bud.* Ram, *Mulk Raj Anand: A Home Appraisal* 43-59.

Brown, J. Mulk Raj Anand: Prophet of Revolution. *Bharat Jyoti* 15 Dec. 1945.

Burra, Edward. Three Views on *Coolie. Kakatiya Journal of English Studies* 2.1 (1977): 226-27 Rpt. in Dhawan, *The Novels of Mulk Raj Anand* 82-83.

Carter, D. Probing Identities: *Untouchable, Things Fall Apart* and *This Earth My Brother. Literary Criterion* 14.3 (1979): 14-29.

Chakravorty, D.K. Gauri and Anasuya: Two Faces of Indian Womanhood. Chakravorty 1-5.

Chandra, Suresh. Social Conscience in the Novels of Mulk Raj Anand. *English Studies in India* (April, 1985): 137-43.

Chatterjee, Debjani. Gandhi s Influence on Anand and His Fiction. *Kakatiya Journal of English Studies* 2.1 (1977): 149-62.

Chaudhury, Jasbir. Images of Women in the Novels of Mulk Raj Anand. *Panjab University Research Bulletin* (Arts) 16.2 (1985): 47-56.

Chetan, Karnani. Mulk Raj Anand The Novelist as a Social Chronicle. *Thought* 24 August 1974: 19-20.

Chellappan, K. The Child Archetype in the Commonwealth Short Stories: Katherine Mansfield, Janet Frane, and Mulk Raj Anand. Dhawan, et al. *Recent Commonwealth Literature* Vol. 1, 60-68.

Chew, Shirley. Fictions of Princely States and Empire. *Ariel* 17.3 (1986): 103-07.

Chinneswara Rao, G.J. Anand s *Private Life of an Indian Prince* and Malgonkar s *The Princes:* A Comparison. *Journal of Indian Writing in English* 4.1 (1976): 15-20.

Cowasjee, Saros. Anand s Princes and Proletarians. *Literary Half-Yearly* 9.2 (1968): 83-104. Rpt. in *Journal of Commonwealth Literature* 5 (1968): 52-64.

. Princes and Politics. *Literary Criterion* 8.4 (1969): 10-18.

. Mulk Raj Anand and His Critics. *Banasthali Patrika* 12 (1969): 57-63.

. Mulk Raj Anand: A Profile. *Illustrated Weekly of India* 4 May 1969.

. Afterword. *Untouchable* by Mulk Raj Anand. Delhi: Orient Paperbacks, 1970.

. Princes and their Collaborators. *Blitz* 1970.

. Mulk Raj Anand s *Coolie:* An Appraisal. *Banasthali Patrika* 8.19 (1972): 8-19. Also in Dhawan, *The Novels of Mulk Raj Anand* 66-77.

. Mulk Raj Anand: The Early Struggle of a Novelist. *Journal of Commonwealth Literature* 7.1 (1972): 49-56.

. Mulk Raj Anand and the B.B.C. *Indian and Foreign Review* 10.10 (1973): 19-20.

. Anand s Literary Creed. *Journal of Indian Writing in English* 1.1 (1973): 66-71. Also in Dhawan, *The Novels of Mulk Raj Anand* 13-18.

. Anand s *Two Leaves and a Bud.□ Indian Literature* 16.3-4 (1973): 134-47.

. Mulk Raj Anand s *Untouchable:* An Appraisal. *Literature East and West* 17. 2-4 (1973): 199-11.

. *The Big Heart:* A New Perspective. *ACLALS Bulletin* 4.2 (1975): 83-86. Rpt. in *Kakatiya Journal of English Studies* 2.1 (1977): 85-92.

. □*The Big Heart:* A Note. Dhawan, *The Novels of Mulk Raj Anand* 140-44.

. Mulk Raj Anand. *Encyclopedia of World Literature in 20th Century.* Wolfgang Bernard Fleischamann. New York: Ungar, 1985.

. Mulk Raj Anand s *The Sword and the Sickle.* *World Literature Written in English* 14.1 (1975): 267-77.

. Mulk Raj Anand: A Hard Road to Fiction. Dwivedi, *Studies in Contemporary Indian Fiction* 82-96.

. The Princes in Indian Fiction. *Kakatiya Journal of English Studies* 2.1 (1977): 48-70.

. Mulk Raj Anand: The Fusion of History and Fiction. McLeod *Subjects Worthy Fame:* 17-26.

Das, J.P. Novels of Mulk Raj Anand. *Indian and Foreign Review* 31 June 1985: 28-29.

Das, G.K. Between Two Heritages: A Note on Mulk Raj Anand s *Confession of a Lover.* *Indian Literary Review* 1.2 (1978): 16-20.

Dayal, B. Mulk Raj Anand: A Spokesman of the Time. Dayal 25-94.

Devarajan, Padmini. Sadharanikarana Elucidated in Anand s *The Bubble.* *Littcrit* 36 & 37, 19. 1-2 (1993): 101-16.

Dhar, T.N. *The Big Heart:* Anand s Novel of Ideas. *Indian Literary Review* 5.3 (Oct. 1987): 33-38.

. Dream, Nightmare, Alternative: The Dialectics of Form in Coolie. Ram, *Mulk Raj Anand: A Home Appraisal* 18-33. ref.: 1542.

. Conscious Raising in a Cultural Frame: The Fiction of Mulk Raj Anand Before 1947. Kaul and Jaidev 135-45.

Dhatwalia, H.R. *The Bubble:* A Study. Ram, *Mulk Raj Anand: A Home Appraisal* 127-38.

Dhawan, R.K. Mulk Raj Anand: *Coolie.* Pradhan 1-22.

. *The Barber s Trade Union:* An Appraisal. *Rajasthan Journal of English Studies* 13 & 14 (1981): 14-19.

Dommergues, A. An Interpretation of Mulk Raj Anand s *Untouchable.* *Commonwealth: Essays and Studies* (France) 8.2 (1985): 14-23.

Dinesh, Kamini. Gauri: Connotations and Eponyms. Kaur 179-86.

Dover, Cedric. The Significance of Anand. *United Asia* 3.6 (1952).

Dulai, Surjit Singh. Practice Before Ideology: Mulk Raj Anand s *Untouchable*. *Journal of South Asian Literature* 27.2 (1992): 187-08.

Dutt, Prabhat Kumar. Mulk Raj Anand in Relation to Tagore, Premchand and Sarat Chatterjee. *Contemporary Indian Literature* Nov.-Dec. 1965.

Dwivedi, S.C. Existentialism in Anand s *Across the Black Waters*. Pathak, *Indian Fiction in English* 25-37.

Fisher, Marlene. Mulk Raj Anand: The Novelist as Novelist. *Panjab University Research Bulletin* (Arts) 4.1 (1973): 257-67.

. The Shape of Lostness: Mulk Raj Anand s Short Stories. *Journal of Indian Writing in English* 2.1 (1974): 1-11.

. Mulk Raj Anand s Confessional Novels. *Journal of Indian Writing in English* 4.2 (1976): 39-45.

. Mulk Raj Anand: A Study of His Confessional Novels. Dwivedi, *Studies in Contemporary Indian Fiction in English* 97-106.

. On Being Seventy Years Young. *Youth Times* 2 Apr. 1976: 10-11.

. Confession of a Lover. *Kakatiya Journal of English Studies* 2.1 (1977): 107-18.

. The Art of Self and the Self of Art: Mulk Raj Anand s *Confession of a Lover: Language Forum* 7.1-4 (1981-1982): 90-100.

. Mulk Raj Anand. *Littcrit* 20 & 21, 11.1-2 (1985): 1-10.

. *The Bubble:* Lightning of the Flame of Life. Dhawan, *The Novels of Mulk Raj Anand.* 216-18.

. Apology for Heroism: Autobiography and Anand. Dhawan, *The Novels of Mulk Raj Anand* 193-02.

. Mulk Raj Anand as Autobiographer. Yaraventelimath *et al.* 177-87.

Gandhi, Lingaraja. Excursion to continental Grave Yard: A Reading Anand s *Across Black Waters*. *Literary Half-yearly* 38-1(1999): 119-29.

Garcia, Irene Santamaria. Mulk Raj Anand: *Coolie* Romulo Gallegos: Canaima: *Hispanic Horizon* 13 (Win 1989).

Gautam, G.L. Indian Renaissance and Reformation: A Comparative Study of Premchand s *Godan* and Mulk Raj Anand s *The Village.* *New Quest* 95, Sep.-Oct. 1992.

. Kashmir: Bonds of Unity. *Patriot* 29 July 1990.

Gemmill, Janet P. The City as Jungle in the Indo-English Novel. Noble and Dutt, 45-67.

Gilman, Marvin. Mulk Raj Anand s Critical Reception: A Reassessment. *Littcrit* 42, 22.1 (1996): 58-68.

Gowda, Anniah H.H. Mulk Raj Anand. *Literary Half-yearly* 6.1 (1965): 51-60. Rpt. as Mulk Raj Anand: A Committed Writer in Prabhakar 69-77.

Goyal, Bhagwat. Mulk Raj Anand: The Writer as Humanist. Goyal, *Culture and Commitment* 70-73.

Gupta, G.S. Balarama. *Untouchable:* A Study. *Contemporary Indian Literature* 7.4 (1967): 12-13.

. The Humanism of Mulk Raj Anand. *Contemporary Indian Literature* 7.3 (1967): 6-8.

. *Coolie* A Prose Epic of Modern India. *Journal of Karnatak University* (Humanities) 12 (1968): 92-99.

. Woman in Anand s Shorter Fiction. *Journal of Karnatak Unviersity* (Humanities) 13 (1969): 188-93.

. Anand s *Big Heart:* A Study. *Banasthali Patrika* 13 (July 1969): 37-43.

. Anand s *Old Woman and the Cow* in Human Perspective. *Journal of Karnatak University* (Humanities) 14 (1970): 143-49.

. Dr Mulk Raj Anand s Prose Poem. *Contemporary Indian Literature* 11.3 (1971): 14-15.

. Towards a Closer Understanding of Anand. Sharma, K.K., *Indo-English Literature* 113-20. ref.: 501. Also in Sharma, K.K., *Perspectives on Mulk Raj Anand* 9-15. ref.: 1546.

. Anand in Letters. *Kakatiya Journal of English Studies* 2 (1977): 210-18.

. Mulk Raj Anand s *Untouchable:* The Dialectics of Self-Affirmation. Naik, *Perspectives* 13-20.

Gupta, Rameshwar. The Gandhi in Anand. Sharma, K.K., *Perspectives on Mulk Raj Anand.* 77-83.

Gupta, Sangeeta. The Nature of Brother-Sister Relationship: *Untouchable, A Bend in the Ganges* and *A Situation in Delhi.* Dhawan, et al. *Recent Commonwealth Literature* Vol. 1. 153-69.

Guruprasad, Thakur. Experimentation with Language in Indo-Anglian Fiction: A Note Towards Definition of Traits in the Works of Mulk Raj Anand. Desai, *Experimentation* 33-80.

Habibullah, E. *Across the Black Waters:* A Novel about Army life. Dhawan, *The Novels of Mulk Raj Anand* 137-39.

Harrex, S.C. Mulk Raj Anand. Harrex, *The Fire and the Offering,* 69-146.

. Quest for Structures: Form, Fable and Technique in the Fiction of Mulk Raj Anand. Sharma, K.K., *Perspectives on Mulk Raj Anand* 153-68.

Henderson, Philip. Mulk Raj Anand. *The Novel Today.* London: Bodley Head, 1936.

Hemenway, Stephen Iqnatius. Mulk Raj Anand. Hemenway Vol. 2. 3-18.

Hirst, Mary Hooper. Mulk Raj Anand. *New Circle* (England) 19.9 (May 1973): 41.

Inamdar, F.A. Twice Born Ananta: *The Big Heart.* Ram, *Mulk Raj Anand: A Home Appraisal* 34-42.

. The Artist and His Beloveds in Mulk Raj Anand s *Morning Face. Commonwealth Review* 6.1 (1994-95): 146-54.

Iyengar, K.R. Srinivasa. Mulk Raj Anand. Iyengar, *Indian Writing in English* 331-57.

. Morning Face. *Kakatiya Journal of English Studies* 2.1 (1977): 239-43.

. *The Bubble:* Not a Routine Work. Dhawan, *The Novels of Mulk Raj Anand* 219-21.

Jaganmohana Chari, A. Outside the Magic Circle: A Study of Anand s *Untouchable. Kakatiya Journal of English Studies* 9 (1988-89): 20-38.

Jha, Pashupati. The Psychology of Superiority and Expression of Anger in Mulk Raj Anand. *Language Forum* 21.1-2 (1995): 56-63. Rpt. in Singh, R.K., *Anger in Action* 56-63.

. Symbol and the Significance: Anand s *Untouchable* and *The Old Women and the Cow.* Srivatsava, R.K., *Symbolism* 50-62.

Jha, Rama. Mulk Raj Anand: The Champion of Gandhian Humanism. Jha 55-86.

Joshi, Krishnanand and B. Shyamala Rao. Mulk Raj Anand as a Novelist. Joshi and Rao 90-99.

Jung, Anees & Dieter Rimenschneider. Mulk Raj Anand s *Death of a Hero.* *Indian Book Chronicle* Mar. 1995: 20.

Kalinnikova, Elena J. The Big-Heart of the Humanist: Mulk Raj Anand. Kalinnikova, *Indo-English Literature: A Perspective* 97-110.

. Leo Tolstoy and Mulk Raj Anand. *Soviet Land* 35.2 (1982): 43.

. Gorkay s Influence on the Creative Work of Mulk Raj Anand. Galik 119 05.

Kandaswami, S. and V.N. Bhat. Mulk Raj Anand s Short Stories on Children *Dyotana* 5.2 (1986): 25-32.

Karnani, Chetan. Mulk Raj Anand: The Novelist as Socialist Chronicler. *Thought* 24 Aug. 1974: 19-20.

Kaul, Jagan Nath. Mulk Raj Anand: A Study. *Literary Studies* (Kashmir) 1947: 60-73.

Kaushik, R.K. From Potter s Wheel to Dragon s Teeth. *Mahfil* 6 (1970): 17-32.

. Red, Brown and Grey Ideological Commitment in Mulk Raj Anand s Novels. Sharma, K.K., *Indo-English Literature* 101-13.

Kher, Indernath. Mulk Raj Anand: Encounter with Dark Passion. *Journal of Indian Writing in English* 11.2 (1983): 3-8.

Klaus, H. Gustav. Zum Beispiel Coolie Ein Vorschlag Zur Eimbeziehung Indo-Englischer Romane in die Betrachtung der. Englischen Literatur des zo Jahrhunderts. *Germanisch romanische Monatschrift* 28, 453-67.

Kohli, Suresh. Anand Sensitive [...] But Lovable. *National Herald, Sunday Herald* 27 Dec. 1981: V.

. Appetite for Words: Mulk Raj Anand. *Link* 4 July 1982: 38.

. □*The Road:* A Fresh Reappraisal. Dhawan, *The Novels of Mulk Raj Anand* 209-10.

Kothari, Sunil. Mulk Raj Anand: A Shining Splendour of Human Life. *Economic Times* 16 Dec. 1979: 4.

Kulshrestha, Chirantan. The Hero as Saviour: Reflections on Anand s *Untouchable.*□ *Journal of Literary Studies* 2.2 (1979): 50-56. *World Literature Written in English* 19.1 (1980): 84-90.

Kumar, Amarendra. □*The Bubble:* A New Form of Fiction. Paniker, *Contemporary Indian Fiction in English* 34 52.

Kumar, Kesaraju. Narrative Technique in *Untouchable* and *Coolie:* A Reading. *Kakatiya Journal*□*of English Studies* 13 (1993): 104-12.

Kumar, Shiv K. Gandhi on Stage: *Little plays of Mahatma Gandhi.*□ Dhawan, *The Novels of Mulk Raj Anand* 225-26.

Kurmanadhan, K. Women Characters in Dr Anand s Novels. *Contemporary Indian Literature* 6.11-12 (1966): 26-27.

. The Novels of Dr Mulk Raj Anand. *Triveni* 36.3 (1967): 50-57.

Latha, K.S. Rural ethos in Indian Novels: Kamala Markandaya s *Nectar in a Sieve,* Raja Rao s *Kanthapura,* Mulk Raj Anand s *The Village.*□ *Triveni* 61.2(1992): 53-56.

Laxmana Murthy, S. Bakha: An Existential Analysis. *Kakatiya Journal of English Studies* 2.1 (1977): 163-75.

Lindsay, Jack. Mulk Raj Anand: Novelist of Changing India. *Our Time* 5.2 (1945). Rpt. as Mulk Raj Anand: A Study in *Contemporary Indian Literature* 5 (1965).

. Mulk Raj Anand. *Kakatiya Journal*□*of English Studies* 2.1 (1977): 1-4.

Mallick, R.P. Mulk Raj Anand in Prince-Land. *Frontier* 29 Dec. 1979: 10-12.

Mathur, O.P. An Approach to the Problem of National Integration in the Novels of Mulk Raj Anand. Sharma, K.K., *Perspectives on Mulk Raj Anand* 115-25.

. Mulk Raj Anand s *Untouchable* and Richard Wright s *Bigger Thomas:* A Comparative Study in Social Protest and

Affirmation. *Literary Half-yearly* 29.2 (1978): 115-28.

. The Hero Between: A Comparative Study of Ngugi s Waiyaki and Anand s Lalu. Narasimhaiah, *Commonwealth Literature* 116-26.

. Narayan s *The Dark Room* and Anand s *The Old Woman and The Cow:* Two modern versions of Sita Myth. *Journal of Commonwealth Literature* 21.1 (1986): 16-25.

Mathur, O.P. and G. Rai. The Early Anand: An Existential Approach. *Rajasthan Journal of English Studies* 13 & 14 (1981): 1-3.

Mehta, P.P. Mulk Raj Anand: The Novelist of the Underdog Mehta, P.P. 139-75.

Mehta, M.L. Anand s *Gauri:* A Study in Feminine Sensibility. *Punjab Journal of English Studies* 5 (1990): 37-52.

. The Exploited Peasant in Indo-English Novel: A Study of Anand s *Village Trilogy*, Markandaya s *Nectar in a Sieve* and Reddy s *The Vultures.* Awasthi 132-46.

Melwani, Murali Das. Approaches to Anand s Short Stories. *Kakatiya Journal of English Studies* 2.1 (1977) 119-24.

Mishra, M.L. Indo-Anglian Literature: Mulk Raj Anand s *Two Leaves and a Bud.* *Modern Review* 143.6 (June 1979): 376-81.

Mukherjee, Arun P. The Exclusive of Post-Colonial Theory and Mulk Raj Anand s *Untouchable:* A Case Study. *Ariel* 22.3 (1991): 27-48.

Mukherjee, Dhurjati. Indo-Anglian Writers: Anand and Bhattacharya. *Society and Commerce* 2.2 (Apr. 1973): 104-05.

Mukherjee, Meenakshi. Beyond *The Village:* An Aspect of Mulk Raj Anand. Naik et al., *Critical Essays* 236-45.

. The Tractor and the Plough: The Contrasted Vision of Sudhin Ghose and Mulk Raj Anand. *Indian Literature* 13.1 (1970): 88-101.

. Who is an Indian Writer ? (Anita Desai and Mulk Raj Anand). *Indian Express* (Mag.) 22 Aug. 1982. 111-18.

Muller, Majan S. Grimm s Sneewittchen and Mulk Raj Anand s The Son of Seven Blind Mothers: Ein Vergleich. *Journal of Karnatak University* (Humanities) 30 (1986): 259-64.

Murti, K.V.S. Theme of Salvation: Mulk Raj Anand and R.K. Narayan. *Triveni* 34 (1965): 50-59. Rpt. in Murti 112-23.

. The Motif of Virtue in Dr Mulk Raj Anand s Novels. *Contemporary Indian Literatures* 6.1 (Jan. 1966).

. Mulk Raj Anand: Chronology. *Contemporary Indian Literature* 5.11-12 (1965): 42-47.

Literature as Soul-Search: A Note on Mulk Raj Anand s Novels: *Journal of English Studies* (Warangal) 4.2 (1972): 272-80.

. Nautchization: Mulk Raj Anand s Novel Technique. *Triveni* 45.2 (1976): 25: 31. Also in Murti 104-11.

. *Seven Summers:* Anand s Fictional Matrix. *Kakatiya Journal of English Studies* 2.1 (1977). Also in Murti 82-92.

Nahal, Chaman. Indian Political Novel: Mulk Raj Anand, Bhabani Bhattacharya and Nayantara Sahgal. Nahal 134-51.

. The Dancers in the Ring: *Little Plays of Mahatma Gandhi* Dhawan, *The Novels of Mulk Raj Anand* 227-29. ref.: 1525.

Naik, M.K. The Plough and the Tractor: The Short Stories of Mulk Raj Anand. *Journal of Karnatak Unviersity* (Humanities) 16 (1972): 91-106.

. The Achievement of Mulk Raj Anand. *Journal of Indian Writing in English* 1.1 (1973): 41-50.

. The Political Novel in Indian Writing in English. *ACLALS Bulletin* 4th Ser. 2 (1975): 33-42.

. Infinite Variety: A Study of the Short Stories of Mulk Raj Anand. Sharma, K.K., *Perspectives on Mulk Raj Anand* 39-51.

Narain, Iqbal and Asha Kaushik. The Democratic Experiment and Social Change in India: Some Perceptions from Mulk Raj Anand. Narain and Luthur 61-77.

Narasimhaiah, C.D. Mulk Raj Anand: The Novel of Human Centrality. Narasimhaiah, *The Swan and the Eagle* 106-34.

Narayan, Shyamala A. Mulk Raj Anand. *Contemporary Novelists* 37-40.

Nasimi, Reza Ahmad. *Untouchable:* Anand s Language of Compassionate Objectivity. Nasimi 5-28.

Nath, Suresh. The Element of Protest in Mulk Raj Anand s Fiction. Sharma, K.K., *Perspectives on Mulk Raj Anand.*

Niranjan, Shiva. The Nature and Extent of Gandhi s Impact on the Early Novels of Mulk Raj Anand and Raja Rao. *Commonwealth Quarterly* 3.2 (1979): 36-66.

Niven, Alastair. Mulk Raj Anand: The Poetry of Protest. *Planet* 8 (Oct.-Nov. 1971): 21-25.

. The Lalu-Trilogy of Mulk Raj Anand. *Literary Half-yearly* 13.1 (1972): 31-49. Rpt. in *Kakatiya Journal of English Studies* 2.1 (1977): 17-38. Also in Walsh, *Readings* 11-26.

. Myth to Moral: Mulk Raj Anand s *The Old Woman and the Cow. ACLALS Bulletin* 4th ser. 3 (1975): 30-38.

Noorusan Bah Begum. Anand s Short Stories. *Contemporary Indian Literature* 12.4 (Oct.-Dec. 1972): 6-11.

Orwell, George. They Throw New Light on India. *Manchester Evening News* 9 Aug. 1945.

. Letter to an Indian. *Tribune* 19 March 1943.

. Selected Notice. *Horizon* (July 1942).

Pachori, Satya S. Anand s *Untouchable:* Bakha s Journey to a Sense of Self-hood. MLA Session on South Asian Literature. Utah: East-West Centre, 1976.

Packham, Gillian. Mulk Raj Anand and the Thirties Movement in England. Sharma, K.K., *Perspectives on Mulk Raj Anand* 52-63.

. Mulk Raj Anand s New Myth. *New Literary Review* 8 (1980): 45-53.

Pallan, Rajesh K. Encounter with the Self: A Study of the Confessional Mode in Mulk Raj Anand s *The Bubble.* Kirpal, *The New Indian Novel,* 11-23.

. The use of Myth in Mulk Raj Anand s *Morning Face.* Ram, *Mulk Raj Anand: A Home Appraisal,* 86-100.

Pant, M.C. Mulk Raj Anand: The Man. *Contemporary Indian Literature* 5.11-12 (Nov.-Dec. 1965).

Parry, Graham, Anand, Orwell and The War. *Language Forum* 7.1-4 (1981-1982): 80-89. Rpt. in Dhawan, *Explorations* 80-90.

Pathak, S.N. Unusual Collocations and Compounds in *Coolie.* Diploma Paper, Central Institute of English and Foreign Languages (Hyderabad), 1973.

Paul, Premila. Anand s *Lament on the Death of a Master of Arts:* A Thematic Analysis. *Journal of Indian Writing in English* 6.2 (1978): 70-76.

. Anand s Awakened Woman: Gauri. *Journal of Annamalai University* (Humanities) 31 (1982): 1-8.

. Major Themes in the Novels of Mulk Raj Anand. Naik, *Perspectives* 1-12.

Pontes, Hilda. The Education of a Rebel: Mulk Raj Anand. *Literary Half-yearly* 27.2 (1986): 105-23.

. Anand s *Untouchable:* A Classic in Experimentation of Theme and Technique. Gupta, *Studies* 128-41.

Prasad, Madhusudan. Conflict in the *The Village.* Ram, *Mulk Raj Anand: A Home Appraisal* 101-10.

Prasad, R. Narendra. Pollution in *Untouchable* and *Scavenger□s Son.□ Littcrit* 11, 6.2 (1980): 32-39.

Prasad, Shaikeswar Sati. *Death of a Hero*: Maqbool Sherwani: The Secular Martyr. Bande, *Victim Consciousness* 17-16.

Pritchett, V.S. The Art of Mr Anand. *London Mercury* 24, 202 (1936).

Raizada, Harish. Ethics and Aesthetics of Mulk Raj Anand. Sharma, K.K., *Perspectives on Mulk Raj Anand* 115-28.

Rajagopalachari, M. and K. Sampath. History and Art in Anand s *Private Life of an Indian Prince.□ Language Forum* 23.1-2 (1997): 79-85.

Rajan, C.K. Myth in Mulk Raj Anand s *Gauri.□ Littcrit* 17.1-2 (1991): 44-55.

Rajan, P.K. *Untouchable* and *Coolie:* A Study in Theme and Form. *Rajasthan Journal of English Studies* 13 & 14 (1981): 89-109. Rpt. as Theme and Form in Mulk Raj Anand s Early Novels in Bhatnagar, *Essays in Criticism.*

. Patterns of Cultural Orientation in the Approach to Indian Reality: A Study Based on the Writings of V.S. Naipaul, E.M. Forster, Nirad C. Chaudhari and Mulk Raj Anand. *Littcrit* 15, 8.2 (1982): 68-109.

. Conflict and Resolution in The Tractor and the Corn Goddess. *Littcrit* 17, 9.2 (1983): 32-38.

. The Lost Child as an Expression of Ambivalent Humanism. Rajan, *Studies* 1-10.

. Conflict of Cultures and Creative Tension in Mulk Raj Anand: A Study Based on Lalu Trilogy. Breitinger and Sarder 163-70.

. Anand s *Lalu Trilogy* and Thakazhi s *Kayar* as Saga Novels. Paniker, *Contemporary Indian Fiction in English* 58-67.

. Psychology of Aggression in Golding s *Lord of Flies* and Anand s *Untouchable.* Rajan, *Studies* 56-62.

. The Theme of the Untouchable in Asan, Anand and Thakazhi. Rajan, *Studies* 63-67.

. Three Heroines: Indulekha, Sita and Gauri: A Study in Feminine Consciousness. *Indian Literature* May-June 1987: 109-18.

. Author as Hero: A Study of *Morning Face.* Dhawan, *The Novels of Mulk Raj Anand* 153-66.

. The Two Voices in *The Old Woman and the Cow. Journal of South-Asian Literature* 26.1 (1991): 277-92.

Ram, Atma. Mulk Raj Anand [...] The Novelist of Rural Life. *Tribune* 12 Dec. 1976.

. Dr Anand: The Novelist of Protest. *Tribune* 11 Dec. 1977.

. Folk Elements in Anand s Novels. Ram, *Essays.* 1-7.

. Anand s Prose Style: An Analysis. Sharma, K.K., *Pespectives on Mulk Raj Anand* 169-76.

. Mulk Raj Anand: The Dozen of Novelists. *Nagpur Times* 6 Jan. 1979.

. Mulk Raj Anand: A Novelist of Revolt. *Tribune* 8 Dec. 1985.

. Some Studies on Mulk Raj Anand. Ram, *Essays* 67-78.

. Anand and the emergence of Indian English. *Advance* May-June 1987: 9-11.

. Mulk Raj Anand: Chronology. *Mulk Raj Anand: A Home Appraisal* 177-230.

. Anand: An Artist of Integrity and Vision. *Advance* Dec. 1989: 19-21.

. The Linguistic Devices in Indian English of Raja Rao and Mulk Raj Anand. Ram, *Essays.*

. The Humanist in Mulk Raj Anand. *Morality in Tess and Other Essays* 55-57.

Ramakrishna, D. Anand s Idea of the Novel. *Kakatiya Journal of English Studies* 2.1 (1977): 190-99.

Rao, A.V. Krishna. Mulk Raj Anand and the Novel of Protest. Rao, A.V. Krishna, *The Indo-English Novel.*

Rao, B. Damodar. Orwell s *Burmese Days* and Anand s *Two Leaves and a Bud:* A Comparative Study. Narasimhaiah, *Commonwealth Literature* 185-02.

. Afterword. *Untouchable* by Mulk Raj Anand. Mysore: Geetha Book House, 1978.

Rao, M. Madhusudan. Anand s Tragic Destinies: An Indian View Ratnam 38-43.

Rao, E. Nageswara. Dialogue in Forster and Anand: A Contrastive Analysis. *Kakatiya Journal of English Studies* 2.1 (1977): 176-89. Rpt. in *Approaches to E.M. Forster: A Centenary Volume.* Ed. V.A. Shahane, Delhi: Arnold Heinemann, 1981. 138-47.

Rao, M. Subba. The Art of Mulk Raj Anand. Rao, M. Subba 141-53.

. Mulk Raj Anand and the Human Condition. Rao, M. Subba 167-83.

. *Two Leaves and a Bud:* An Empathetic Study. Rao, M. Subba 184-95.

Rao, P. Raghavendra. Mulk Raj Anand. Raghavacharyulu, *The Two-Fold Voice* 88-98.

Reddy, K. Venkata. Anand s *Lament on the Death of a Master of Arts:* A Study. *Journal of Indian Writing in English* 5.2 (1977): 28-35.

. Cruelty of Man to Man: Mulk Raj Anand s *Two Leaves and a Bud.* *Kakatiya Journal of English Studies* 8 (1987-88): 49-59.

. Why Don t I Die?: *Coolie.* Reddy, K. Venkata, *Major Indian Novelists* 7-15.

Reddy, T. Vasudeva. Expression of Anger in Mulk Raj Anand s *Two Leaves and a Bud.* *Language Forum* 21-1-2 (1995): 75-80.

Renuka, E. Three Women at the Cross-roads: A Note on Man-Woman Relationship in Three Indian Novels [R.K. Narayan s *The Dark Room,* Anand s *Gauri* and Ranganayakamma s *Janaki Vimukthi* (Telugu)] *Kakatiya Journal of English Studies* 17 (1997): 103-10.

Rickwood, Edgell. Mulk Raj Anand. *Socialist* 2.8 (1937).

. Three Views on *Coolie.* *Kakatiya Journal of English Studies* 2.1 (1977): 223-25. Also in Dhawan, *The Novels of Mulk Raj Anand* 78-79.

Riemenschneider, Dieter. An Ideal Man in Mulk Raj Anand s Novels. *Indian Literature* 10.1 (1966): 29-51.

. The Function of Labour in Mulk Raj Anand s Novels. *Journal of the School of Languages* (1976): 1-20.

. Mulk Raj Anand: *Confession of a Lover.* *World Literature Written in English* 16.1 (1977): 105-09. Also in *Indian Author* 2.1 (1977): 73-76.

. *Death of a Hero.* *Kakatiya Journal of English Studies* 2.1 (1977): 235-38. Rpt. as *Death of a Hero:* The Problem of the Meaning of Life. in Dhawan, *The Novels of Mulk Raj Anand* 222-24.

. Alienation in the Novels of Mulk Raj Anand. Sharma, K.K., *Perspectives on Mulk Raj Anand* 94-114.

. Mulk Raj Anand. *Edition Text und Kritix.* Munchen: 4 Nig, 1984: 17.

. Mulk Raj Anand Bock and Wertheim 173-89.

. Mulk Raj Anand, Anita Desai, G.V. Desani, P. Lal, Kamala Markandaya, R.K. Narayan, Raja Rao, Salman Rushdie and Khushwant Singh. *Lexikon der Weit Literatur.* Dortmund: Harenberg Kommunikation, 1988.

. *Untouchable, Coolie, The Old Woman, and the Cow. Kindlers Literatur Lexikon,* Vol. I, Munchen: Kindler Verlag, 1988.

. *The Bubble:* A Literary Achievement. Dhawan, *The Novels of Mulk Raj Anand* 211-15.

Robertson, R.T. *Untouchable* as an Archetypal Novel. *World Literature Written in English* 142. (1975): 239-45.

S.K.R. The Garden Coolie. *New Statesman and Nation* 14 (1937) ms. 332.

Sahay, Vikas Mohan. Social Prophetism in Anand s *Untouchable. Orbit. Journal of Literature in English* (Gaya, Bihar) 1997: 83-87.

Sanjay. The Lost Child An Appreciation. *Mother India* Aug. 1973: 648-49.

Sanyal, S.C. Mulk Raj Anand: His Stylistic Devices. Sanyal, *English Language in India* 69-77. Appendix.

Saxena, O.P. M.R. Anand: Art Critic and Novelist. Saxena *Glimpses* Vol. 3. 159-71.

Sethi, Vijay Mohan. The Theme of the Idiocy of Feudal Lords in Anand s Shorter Fiction. Ram, *Mulk Raj Anand: A Home Appraisal* 139-48.

. The Lost Child: Anand s Stories at a Glance. Sethi 71-76.

. Mulk Raj Anand and Silent Sufferers. Sethi 7-12.

. A Lesson in Compassion. Sethi 77-80.

Sharma, Ashok Kumar. Native Consciousness in Anand s Short Stories. *Language Forum* 19.2 (1993): 151-59.

Sharma, Atma Ram. Folk Elements in Anand s Novels. *Kakatiya Journal of English Studies* 2.1 (1977): 200-09.

Sharma, I.K. *Untouchable: Lava of Love. Language Forum* 21.1-2 (1995): 70-74.

Sharma, K.K. Introduction. Sharma, K.K., *Perspectives on Mulk Raj Anand* IX-XXXI.

. My Hunches about the Novel: Mulk Raj Anand s Theory of Fiction, *Kakatiya Journal of English Studies* 3 (1978): 225-52.

Sharma, Govind N. Anand s Englishmen: The British Presence in the Novels of Mulk Raj Anand. *World Literature Written in English* 21.2 (1982): 336-41.

Sharma, Sudharshan. Gandhian Ideology and Mulk Raj Anand. Sharma Sudharshan, *The Influence of Gandhian Ideology* 21-42.

Sharma, Tara Chand. Bakha s Struggle in *Untouchable.* Ram, *Mulk Raj Anand: A Home Appraisal* 1-17.

Shepherd, Ron. Alienated Being: A Reappraisal of Anand s Alienated Hero Sharma, K.K., *Perspectives on Mulk Raj Anand* 139-52.

Shivpuri, Jagadish. Tagore and Anand. Sharma, K.K., *Perspectives on Mulk Raj Anand* 84-93.

. *The Village:* The Emergence of a Hero. Dhawan, *The Novels of Mulk Raj Anand* 110-17.

. *Across the Black Waters:* The Hero Crosses the Muteness of Obedience. Dhawan, *The Novels of Mulk Raj Anand* 126-36.

. *The Sword and the Sickle:* The Dynamic of Favourable Circumstances. Dhawan, *The Novels of Mulk Raj Anand* 167-81.

. Mulk Raj Anand s *The Road:* An Interpretation *Littcrit* 22 & 23 12.1-2 (1986): 19-26. Also in Dhawan, *The Novels of Mulk Raj Anand* 203-08.

. *The Big Heart:* The Gathering of the Crows. *Kakatiya Journal of English Studies* 3 (1978): 213-24. Also in Dhawan, *The Novels of Mulk Raj Anand* 144-52.

Singh, Amarjit. Why are Anand s Later Novels Unsuccessful? *Commonwealth Quarterly* 4.13 (1979): 68-70.

. *The Private Life of an Indian Prince* as a Novel of Protest. *Commonwealth Quarterly* 13.37 (1988): 1-16.

Singh, Manmohan. Marxian View of the British Raj in Anand. Srivastava, R.K., *Colonial Consciousness* 95-106.

Singh, Mina Surjit. *Female Perspective in the Fiction of Mulk Raj Anand* Singh, Sushla 147-53.

Singh, R. Bhagwan. Victim Consciousness in the Early Novels of Mulk Raj Anand. Bande, *Victim Consciousness* 1-6.

Singh, R.S. From Resentment to Social Protest: Mulk Raj Anand. Singh, R.S. *Indian Novel in English.* 38-54.

Singh, Satyanarain. Yoke of Pity: The Poet in Anand s Novels. *Kakatiya Journal of English Studies* 2.1 (1977): 125-48.

Singh, Sunaina. Protest in the Novels of Mulk Raj Anand. *Osmania Journal of English Studies* 17.1 (1981): 123-34.

Singh, Tajinder. Elements of the Bildungsroman in *Coolie.*□ *Punjab Journal of English Studies* (1986): 115-27.

Singh, Veera, The Slave Rebel: A Closer Look at Untouchability. *Indian Literature* Sep.-Oct. 1982: 123-33.

Sinha, K.N. Existentialism in Mulk Raj Anand s *Lament on the Death of a Master of Arts* Sinha, *Indian Writing in English* 10-18.

. The Mythic Parallel: A Study in Anand s Later Fiction. Prasad, Hari Mohan *Response* 63-79.

Sinha, Ravinandan. Expression of Anger in Anand s *The Sword and the Sickle.* *Language Forum* 21.1-2 (1995): 64-69.

Sivadasan, C.P. Mulk Raj Anand s *Untouchable* and Thakazhi s *The Scavenger□s Son:* Some Similarities. Paniker *Contemporary Indian Fiction in English* 53-57.

Sood, S.C. The Other Side of *Untouchable.* *Creative Forum* 1.1 (1989): 13-27.

. The Return of the Prodigal: A Reading of Mulk Raj Anand s *Untouchable.* *Commonwealth Quarterly* 14.39 (1989): 34-49.

Srinath, C.N. Pariah at Cross-Roads: Image as Symbol of Regeneration. Srinath, 70-84.

Steinvorth, Klaus. Mulk Raj Anand s *Private Life of an Indian Prince* and Manohar Malgonkar s *The Princes.* *Literary Half-yearly* 14.1 (1973): 76-91.

Stilz, Gerhard. Experiments in Squaring of the Ellipsis: A Critical Reading of the Autobiographies of Gandhi, Nehru, Chauduri and Anand Yaranintelimath *et al.* 162-76.

Sudhakar, Premila Paul. Major Themes in the Novels of Mulk Raj Anand. Naik, *Perspectives* 1-12.

Sundaram, P.S. Single and Double Vision: Anand, Raja Rao, and Narayan. *Rajasthan University Studies in English* 7 (1974): 68-78.

Tagore, Leo. Social Justice in Anand s *Coolie* and Achebe s *Things Fall Apart.* Dhawan, *The Novels of Mulk Raj Anand* 84-97.

Tarinayya, M. *Untouchable:* An Analysis. *Journal of Mysore University* (Arts) 26 (1969): 22-45.

Tasneem, N.S. Mulk Raj Anand and New Humanism. *Advance* Dec. 1985: 6-7, 9.

Tharu, Susie. Decoding Anand s Humanism. *Kunapipi* 4 (1982): 30-42.

. Reading against the Imperial Grain: Inter-texuality, Narrative Structure and Literal Humanism in Mulk Raj Anand s *Untouchable. Jadhavapur Journal of Comparative Literature* 24 (1986): 60-71.

Thomas, O.J. The Enslaved and the Unsolved: The Characters of Anand and Anita Desai. *Quest* (Ranchi) 12.1 (1998): 39-43.

Thomas, T.K. The Hindu Ethos A Novelist s Perspective. *Religion and Society* 20.4 (Dec. 1973): 54-71.

Tupikova, Y. Mulk Raj Anand. *Soviet Literature* 9 (1953).

Vakeel, Hilda, Three Views on *Coolie. Kakatiya Journal of English Studies* 2.1 (1977): 228-31. Also in Dhawan, *The Novels of Mulk Raj Anand* 79-81.

Varalakshmi, P. Mulk Raj Anand s *Lament on the Death of a Master of Arts:* An Analysis. *Journal of Indian Writing in English* 7.2 (1979): 82-87.

Varma, Ravi S. Hindustani Words in Mulk Raj Anand. A paper presented at XI All India Conference of Dravidian Linguists, 5-7 June 1981. Dept. of Linguistics, Osmania University, Hyderabad.

Venugopal, C.V. The Short Stories of Mulk Raj Anand: A Study. *Journal of Karnatak University* (Humanities) 15 (1971): 145-56.

. Munoo and Mrs Mainwaring: A Note on the Last Chapter of *Coolie. Journal of Karnatak University* (Humanities) 29 (1975): 110-16.

. Bakha s Deliverance: A Consideration of the Last Part of Anand s *Untouchable. Journal of Karnatak University* 21 (1977): 106-10.

Verghese, C. Paul. Raja Rao, Mulk Raj Anand, Narayan and Others. *Indian Writing Today* 3.1 (1969): 31-38.

. The Proletarian Humour of Mulk Raj Anand. Verghese, *Problems* 127-32.

Verma, K.D. Understanding Mulk Raj Anand. An Introduction. *South Asian Review* 15.12 (July, 1991): 1-11.

. Ideological Confrontation and Synthesis in Mulk Raj Anand s *Conversations in Bloombury.* *Journal of South Asian Literature* 28.1 (1995): 181-204.

. Mulk Raj Anand: A Reappraisal. *Indian Literature* 72, Mar.-Apr. 1996: 150-65.

Verma, Urmila. Thematic Concerns and Artistic Devices in *Morning Face* Ram, *Mulk Raj Anand: A Home Appraisal* 76-85.

Walsh, William. Mulk Raj Anand. *Contemporary Novelists* 5th ed. 37-40.

. Some Observations on Mulk Raj Anand s Fiction. Sharma, K.K., *Perspective on Mulk Raj Anand* 177-80.

Wasi, Jchanara. The Big Heart at Eighty. *Link* 15 Dec. 1985: 33-34.

. Focus on Two Writers. *Economics Times* 2 Oct. 1988: 4.

Weir, Ann Lowry. Style and Range in New English Literatures (re: R.K. Narayan, Mulk Raj Anand and V.S. Naipaul). Kachru 283-93.

Williams, Haydn Moore. Mulk Raj Anand: Realism and Politics. *Miscellany* 55, Feb. 1972: 9-42.

Xavier, M.J.N.A. L humanisme de Mulk Raj Anand, Dans Ses Romans. *Journal of Karnatak University* (Humanities) 14 (1970): 197-206.

Zaheer, Sajjad. Mulk Raj Anand. *Contemporary Indian Literature* 5. 11-12 (1965).

Zaheer, Sajjad. The Future of the PWA Movement (Mulk Raj Anand). *Contemporary Indian Literature* 7.1 (1967).

V. Reviews

All Men are Brother. Rev. of *The Sword and the Sickle, Times Literary Supplement* 3 Jan. 1942: 4.

Asnani, Shyam M. Rev. of *Across the Black Waters, Commonwealth Quarterly* 9. 28 (1984): 46-49.

Bandopadhyay, Manohar. Rev. of *Untouchable. Patriot* 18 Apr. 1982: 2-3.

Bartholomew, R.L. A Disappointing Autobiography. Rev. of *Seven Summers. Thought* 17 May 1952: 15-16.

Berry, Margaret. Bhikhu and Kabir: The Untouchable and the Saint. Rev. of *The Road. CRNLE Review Journal* (Winter), 1988.

Brown, F.J. Rev. of *The Big Heart. Life and Letters Today* XLVII. 99, 1945.

Burra, Edward. Rev. of *Coolie. Kakatiya Journal of English Studies* 2.1 (1977): 226-27. Notes, Rpt. from *Spectator* 5635 (1935).

Calder-Marshall. Rev. of *Two Leaves and a Bud. Left Review* 3.1 (1931).

. Rev. of *Across the Black Waters. Life and Letters Today* 28.4 (1941).

Chander, K.M. Rev. of *Panorama: An Anthology of Indian Short Stories. Literary Criterion* 23.4 (1988): 95-97.

Clare, Tullis. Rev. of *The Sword and the Sickle. Time and Tide* 33.17 (1942).

Collis Maurice. Rev. of *Across the Black Waters. Time and Tide* 21.48 (1940).

Cowasjee, Saros. Rev. of *Morning Face. Indian Literature* 13.1 (1970).

. Rev. of *Two Leaves and a Bud. Indian Literature* 16.3-4 (1973).

. Rev. of *The Sword and the Sickle. World Literature Written in English* 14.2 (1975): 267-77.

. Rev. of *Confession of a Lover. International Fiction Review* 4.1 (1977). Also in *Journal of Commonwealth Literature* 12.1 (1977): 75-76.

Das, Kamala. Rev. of *Confession of a Lover. Youth Times* Sep. 1976.

Davies, Rhys. Rev. of *The Village. Life and Letters Today* 21.22 (1939).

Dewsbury, Ronald. Rev. of *Coolie. Life and Letters Today* Vol. XV, No. 5. 1936.

Dhawan, R.K. Rev. of *The Barber□s Trade Union. Rajasthan Journal of English Studies* 13 & 14 (1981): 14-19.

Dobree, Bonamy. Rev. of *Across the Black Waters. Spectator* 22 Nov. 1940.

Dover, Cedric. Rev. of *Coolie. Congress Socialist* 1.35 (1936).

Duncan, Margaret. Boy-Man Complexities Rev. of *Morning Face. Times* 2 Mar. 1969: V. Weekly Review.

Eastern Approaches. Rev. of *The Private Life of an Indian Prince. Times Literary Supplement:* Aug. 21 (1953): 533.

English and Indian. Rev. of *Two Leaves and a Bud. Times Literary Supplement* 15 May 1937: 379.

Fisher, Marlene. Rev. of *Confession of a Lover. Books Abroad* 50.4 (1976): 953.

. Rev. of *Between Tears and Laughter. World Literature Today* 16.3 (1992): 581-82.

Gandhi, Lingaraja. Did the Sun Shine in Heaven Also. Rev. of *Between Tears and Laughter. Literary Half-yearly* 35.1 (1994): 162-64.

Gupta, G.S. Balarama. Rev. of *Morning Face. Journal of Karnatak University* (Humanities) 13 (1969): 204-06.

Gupta, L.N. Rev. of *Confession of a Lover. Hitvada* 7 Mar. 1976.

Hawkins, Desmond. Rev. of *Across the Black Waters. New Statesman and Nation* 20.509 (n.s.) (1940).

India At War Rev. of *Across the Black Waters. Times Literary Supplement* 7 Sep. 1946: 456.

Indian Childhood Rev. of *Seven Summers. Times Literary Supplement* 28 Dec. 1951: 833.

Iyengar, K.R. Srinivasa. We Belong to Suffering [...] Rev. of *Coolie. Deccan Herold* 5 Nov. 1952.

. Rev. of *Confession of a Lover. Journal of Indian Writing in English* 4.2 (1976): 75-78.

. Rev. of *Morning Face. Kakatiya □Journal of English Studies* 2.1 (1977): 239-43.

. Unusual Achievement. Rev. of *The Bubble. Indian Literature* Jan.-Feb. 1985: 113-19.

Jacob, Jessica. Touching Humdrum. Rev. of *Between Tears and Laughter. Times of India* July 1973: 11.

Kapadia, Novy. Rev. of *Across The Black Waters. Link* 19 Apr. 1981: 40.

Kapur, Kamala. From the Complex to the Simple. Rev. of *The Village. Times Literary Supplement* 18 Sep. 1977: 1010.

. Rev. of *The Village. Times of India* 18 Sept. 1977: 10.

Kaushik, R.K. Indian Princes Again. Rev. of *The Private Life of an Indian Prince. Literary Half-yearly* 12.1 (1971): 107-12.

Khare, Randhir. Rev. of *Two Leaves and a Bud. Indian P.E.N.* 41 (Feb. 1975): 24-25.

Kohli, Suresh. Rev. of *Morning Face. Indian and Foreign Review* 7.23 (1970): 20-21.

Krishna, Francine. Love in the Twenties. Rev. of *The Old Woman and the Cow. Quest* 99, Jan.-Feb. 1976: 90-91.

Malhotra, Indu. Rev. of *Confession of a Lover. Times of India* (Mag) 9 Dec. 1976: 10.

McDowell, Judith H. Rev. of *Morning Face. World Literature Written in English* 9 (1970).

Mehta, Boman, Rev. of *Untouchable. Scrutiny* 4.1 (1935).

Melwani, Murali Das. Rev. of *Between Tears and Laughter. Journal of Indian Writing in English* 2.2 (1974): 62-64.

Menon, K.P.S. Ennoblement via Tragedy . Rev. of *The Private Life of an Indian Prince. Times of India* 21 Feb. 71: 10.

Murti, K.V.S. Rev. of *Confession of a Lover. Triveni* 46.1 (1977): 130-32.

N.G.M. Rev. of *The Old Woman and the Cow. Indian P.E.N.* 27, June 1961.

Nahal, Chaman. Rev. of *Confession of a Lover. Indian Literature* 20.1 (1977): 90-83.

Naik, M.K. Rev. of *Between Tears and Laughter. Littcrit* 38, 20.1 (1994): 94-97.

Naikar, Basavaraj S. Rev. of *Between Tears and Laughter. Century* 4 May 1974: 13-14.

Nandakumar, Prema. Rev. of *The Bubble. Journal of Indian Writing in English* 13.1 (1985): 103-06.

. Many-Layered Exuberance. Rev. of *The Bubble. Indian Literary Review* 3.2 (1985): 80-83.

Niven, Alastair. A Modern Indian Intellect. Rev. of *Morning Face and The Private Life of an Indian Prince. Journal of Commonwealth Literature* 6.1 (1971): 129-31.

. Commitment to Humanity. Rev. of *The Bubble. Book Review* Jan.-Feb. 1985: 14-15.

. A Novel of Self-Revelation: Anand s Enduring Bubble. Rev. of *The Bubble. Indian Book Chronicle* Jan. 1991: 3-4.

O Brien, Kate. Rev. of *The Sword and the Sickle. Spectator* 5938 (1942).

. Rev. of *The Village. Spectator* 5783 (1939).

Orwell, George. Rev. of *The Sword and the Sickle. Horizon* (1942). Rpt. in *The Collected Essays, Journalism and Letters of George Orwell* 11. Eds. Sonia Orwell and Ian Angus. London: Secker & Warburg. 1968.

Pandit, Manorama. Rev. of *The Road. World Literature Written in English* 14.2 (1975): 421.

Palmer, Arnold. Mr Anand s Novel. Rev. of *Two Leaves and a Bud. London Mercury* May 1937.

Perles, Alfred. Rev. of *The Barber s Trade Union and Other Stories. Life and Letters Today* XLII (1944).

Pritchett, V. Rev. of *Coolie. Commonwealth Review* 6.1 (1994-95): 173-74.

Quennell, Peter. Rev. of *Coolie. New Statesman and Nation* 12.28 (n.s.) 1936.

Raina, M.L. Rev. of *Confession of a Lover. Indian Book Chronicle* Jan. 1977: 40.

. A Search for form. Rev. of *The Bubble. Indian Book Chronicle* 1 May 1984: 161.

Rees, Goronwy. Rev. of *Two Leaves and a Bud. Spectator* 5679 (1937).

Reuben, Elizabeth. *Rev. of Panorama. Indian Express* 5 July 1987: 11.

Rev. of *Untouchable. Times Literary Supplement* 2 May 1935: 289.

Rev. of *The Village. Times Literary Supplement* 15 Apr. 1939: 215.

Rev. of *The Sword and the Sickle. Times Literary Supplement* 2 May 1942: 221.

Rev. of *Coolie. Times Literary Supplement* 20 June 1936: 520.

Rev. of *The Barber□s Trade Union and Other Stories. Times Literary Supplement* 1 July 1944: 317.

Rickword, Edgell. Rev. of *Coolie. Kakatiya Journal of English Studies* 2.1 (1977): 223-25. Notes.

Riemenschneider, Dieter. Rev. of *Confession of a Lover. World Literature Today* 16.1 (1977): 105-09.

Rev. of *The Bubble. Littcrit* 18, 10.1 (1984): 62-65.

S.D. Fancy and Fact. Rev. of *The Private Life of an Indian Prince. Thought* 10 Apr. 1954: 12.

S.M. Rev. of *Gauri. Democratic World* 18 July 1976: 16.

Singh, Khushwant. A Delightful Autobiography. Rev. of *The Bubble. Illustrated Weekly of India* 19-25 (1984): 34-35.

. Good Guys, Bad Guys and Mulkees. Rev. of *Morning Face. Times of India* 13 July 1969: IV.

Singh, Madhu. Rev. of *The Tractor and the Corn Goddess and Other Stories. Indian Book Chronicle* Nov.-Dec. 1987: 305.

. Rev. of *Death of a Hero. Indian Book Chronicle* July 1988: 177-78.

Singh, Narendra Pal. A Punjabi Response. Rev. of *Across the Black Waters. Indian Literary Review* No. 10 (1978-79): 34-36.

Stoll, Dennis Gray. Rev. of *The Barber□s Trade Union. Aryan Path* Jan. 1945: 36.

Spender, Stephen. Rev. of *Two Leaves and a Bud. Life and Letters Today* 14.8 (1937).

Sunderarajan, P.K. Rev. of *Coolie. West Coast Review* 7.2 (1972).

Tales of Indians. Rev. of *Across the Black Waters. Times Literary Supplement* 7 Dec. 1940: 619.

Vakeel, Hilda. Rev. of *Coolie. Kakatiya Journal of English Studies* 2.1 (1977) 228-31. Notes.

Venugopal, C.V. Rev. of *Confession of a Lover. Journal of Karnatak University* (Humanities) (1977): 189-90.

Verghese, Paul. Self-Portrait. Rev. of *Morning Face. Quest* 63, Aug. 1973: 103-04.

West, Anthony. Rev. of *The Village. New Statesman and Nation* 27.425 (n.s.) 1939.

Zuckerman, Ruth Van Horn. Rev. of *Lament on the Death of a Master of Arts. Books Abroad* 42.2 (1968): 487.

VI. Dissertations

Agarwal, Balaram Prasad. Mulk Raj Anand: A Study of Miseries, Struggles and Splendours in his Fiction. Ravishankar U, 1980.

Agnihotri, Gopinath. On the Treatment of Indian Life and Problems in the Novels of M.R. Anand, Raja Rao and R.K. Narayan. Meerut U, 1973. Meerut: Shalabh Book House, 1984, 1993.

Ahmad, Reja. Fictional Structures: A Stylistic study of the Fiction of R.K. Narayan, Mulk Raj Anand and Anita Desai. U of Bihar.

Badve, V.V. Narrative Techniques in Indian Fiction in English with Particular Reference to the Work of Raja Rao, R.K. Narayan, M.R. Anand and Manohar Malgonkar. Shivaji U, 1979.

Balaram, Chaswal. The Stylistic Development of Mulk Raj Anand. Central Institute of English and Foreign Languages (Hyderabad), 1973.

Bamezai, Geeta. Social and Moral Concerns in the Journalistic and Creative Writings of Mulk Raj Anand. Banaras Hindu U, 1989.

Bhaskaran, V.H. The Theme of Social Justice in the Novels of Mulk Raj Anand and Bhabani Bhattacharya. U of Madurai, 1989.

Bhat V. Nithanatha. Themes and Techniques in the Short Stories of Mulk Raj Anand, Raja Rao and R.K. Narayan. Calicutt U, 1988.

Bhatt, P.N. A Thematic Study of the Novels of R.K. Narayan, Mulk Raj Anand, Manohar Malgonkar. Saurashtra U, 1978.

Chowdhury, Beni Madhav. Political Strain in the Novels of Mulk Raj Anand. Bihar U.

Damodar Rao, B. Social and Political Awareness in the Novels of Mulk Raj Anand and George Orwell. U of Mysore, 1980.

Dayal, Barameshwar. Critical Study of the Themes and Techniques of the Indo-Anglian Short Story Writers with Special Reference to Mulk Raj Anand, R.K. Narayan and K.A. Abbas. Magadh U (Bodh Gaya), 1984. Ranchi: Jubilee Prakashan, 1985.

Desai, Achala Arun Kumar. The Autobiographical Novels of Mulk Raj Anand: A Study. Karnatak U, 1990.

Devasia, S.D. Indian English and the Indian Spirit: Analysis of Three Novelists: R.K. Narayan, Raja Rao and Mulk Raj Anand. Diss. (M.A.). U of Calicut, 1979.

George, C.J. The Artist as Social Critic. A Study of Mulk Raj Anand s Major Novels. North Eastern Hill U, 1983.

Gulati, Vinod Bhusan. Mulk Raj Anand s Novels: A Study in Narrative Technique. Meerut U, 1983.

Gupta, Balarama. The Artist as Humanist: A Study of M.R. Anand s Fiction. U of Karnatak (Dharwad), 1970.

Gupta, Shravan Kumar. Tradition and Modernity in the Novels of Mulk Raj Anand. Meerut U, 1982.

Jacob, Susan. Women in Mulk Raj Anand s Fiction. Diss. (M.Phil.), U of Annamalai, 1982.

Juneja, Om Prakash. Colonial Consciousness in Recent Black American, Indian and African Fiction with Special Reference to the Novels of Richard Wright, Ralph Ellison, James Baldwin, Raja Rao, R.K. Narayan, M.R. Anand, Chinua Achebe, T.M. Aluko and James Ngugi. Maharaja Sayaji Rao U of Baroda, 1980.

Kaushik, Raj Kumar. Mulk Raj Anand A Committed Artist. U of Delhi, 1968.

Kaur, Matania Din. Moral Vision in the Novels of Mulk Raj Anand Diss. (M.Phil.), Panjab U, 1992.

Khan, S.A. The Novel of Commitment: A Study of Mulk Raj Anand. U of Marathwada (Beed), 1988.

Kulothungan. Anand s *Gauri* and Narayan s *The Dark Room:* A Comparative Study. Diss. (M.Phil.), Annamalai U.

Kumar, Birendra. Social Conflict in the Novels of Mulk Raj Anand. Magadh U, 1988.

Mehar, Amarjit Singh. Artist as Rebel: Protest in Mulk Raj Anand s Novels. Panjab U, 1983.

Mishra, D.S. Novels of Mulk Raj Anand: A Reappraisal. Kashi Vidyapith.

Misra, Lalji, The Impact of Gandhi on Indian English Fiction with Special Reference to M.R. Srivastava, R.K. Narayan, Anand and Raja Rao Diss. (D.Phil.), Gyanpur, 1992.

Narlikar, Arun. An Examination of Mulk Raj Anand s Novels with Particular Reference to His Themes, Characterization and Techniques. Saugar U, 1980.

Oberoi, Narenda Kumar. Sociology of Indo-English Novel with Special Reference to the Novels of Mulk Raj Anand, R.K. Narayan, Raja Rao. Panjab U, 1980.

Periyanyaki, Premila. The Novels of Mulk Raj Anand: A Thematic Study. Annamalai U, 1981.

Perkins, Susan Havard. Reflections of Modern Culture in Indo-Anglian Literature: Illustrations from the Novels of R.K. Narayan and Mulk Raj Anand. U of California, 1957.

Prasad, Shaileshwar Sati. Social Realism in the Novels of Mulk Raj Anand. Patna U, 1981.

Rajan, C.K. Language of Fictional Writings of Mulk Raj Anand. Kerala U, 1987.

Rajan, P.K. Humanistic Ambivalence in the Novels of Mulk Raj Anand: A Dialectical Approach. Kerala U, 1990.

Rao, A.V. Krishna. The Indo-Anglian Novel and the Changing Tradition: A Study of the Novels of M.R. Anand, Kamala Markandaya, R.K. Narayan and Raja Rao. U of Mysore, 1964. Rao and Raghavan, 1972.

Rao, M. Prathapa. Mulk Raj Anand s Trilogy: A Study. Diss. (M.Phil.), Nagarjuna U, 1983.

Reeta. Woman Characters in Mulk Raj Anand s Novels: A Psychological Interpretation. U of Himachal Pradesh, 1990.

Ruebeling, Heinrich. Die Stellung des Romans *Private Life of an Indian Prince* in Gesam Twerk des Autors Mulk Raj Anand. Diss. (M.Phil.), U of Johann Wolfgang Grethe Universtat, 1984.

Satyanarayana N. New Morality in Indian English Fiction with Special Reference to Anand, Narayan and Arun Joshi. Kakatiya U, 1989.

Sethi, Vijay Mohan. Short Stories of M.R. Anand: A Critical Study. U of Himachal Pradesh, 1989. New Delhi: Ashish Publishing House, 1990.

Sharma, A. Kumar. The Theme of Exploitation in the Novels of Mulk Raj Anand. Meerut U, 1986. New Delhi: H.K. Publishers, 1990.

Sharma, T.C. Mulk Raj Anand: The Art of Characterization. Himachal Pradesh U, 1985.

Shepherd, Ronald. Aspects of Identity in the Indo-English Novel: A Study of Three Novelists: Raja Rao, R.K. Narayan, and M.R. Anand. U of Adelaide, 1974.

Singh, Jaipal. Themes and Techniques in the Novels of Mulk Raj Anand. Rohilkhand U, 1988.

Singh, M. Mulk Raj Anand: A Study of the Malcontents in His Novels. Banaras Hindu U, 1985.

Subhana, Asma. A Comparative Study of Fictional Speech in E.M. Forster, M.R. Anand, Robin White and Alan Pafoti. Diss. (M.Phil.), Osmania U, 1988.

Suresh Kumar, A.V. Non-Indian Characters: Anglo-American and European in the Novles of Mulk Raj Anand, Raja Rao, R.K. Narayan, B. Rajan, Markandaya and Anita Desai. Osmania U, 1991.

Suryanarayana Murti, K.V. *The Sword and the Sickle:* A Study of Mulk Raj Anand s Novels. Andhra U, 1972. Mysore: Geeta Book House, 1983.

Swarup, Hem Lata. Mulk Raj Anand: A Critical Survey. U of Agra, 1970.

Tara Chand. Protest in the Five Novels of Mulk Raj Anand. Himachal Pradesh U, 1985.

Thakur, V.R. East and West: Indo-Anglian Novel with Special Reference to Mulk Raj Anand, Kamala Markandaya, Manohar Malgonkar. Bombay U, 1985.

Upvinder Kaur. Patterns of Linguistics Variation in Social Context in Mulk Raj Anand s *Coolie*.□ Punjabi U, 1990.

Contributors

Binod Mishra. Department of Languages, BITS, Pilani, Rajasthan.

Shiv Kumar Yadav. Lecturer, Department of English, G.D. College, Begusarai, Bihar.

Ashok Kumar Bachchan. Reader in English, L.N. Mithila University, Darbhanga, Bihar.

U.S. Rukhaiyar. Pro-Vice Chancellor (Retd.), J.P. University, Chapra, Bihar.

Ramesh Kumar Gupta. Research Scholar, Department of English, Jai Prakash University, Chapra, Bihar.

D. Ramakrishna. Department of English, Kakatiya University, Warangal, Andhra Pradesh.

T.M.J. Indra Mohan. Professor, Post-graduate and Research Department of English, Pachaiyappa s College, Chennai, Tamil Nadu.

N.P. Ravi Kumar. Professor of English, Post-graduate and Research Department of English, Pachaiyappa s College, Chennai, Tamil Nadu.

Evangeline Manickam. Professor of English, Department of Humanities and Social Sciences, Indian Institute of Technology, Chennai, Tamil Nadu.